Vit Horky

# CUSTOMER SERVICE IN THE TRANSHUMAN AGE

Prague, 2018

Vit Horky

Customer Service in the Transhuman Age

Published by: Brand Embassy Ltd, odštěpný závod,

Rohanské nábřeží 678/25, 186 00 Prague 8, Czech Republic

First edition, 2018

ISBN 9781731082152

*The bible said that god made man in his own image.*
*The German philosopher Ludwig Feuerbach said that man*
*made God in his own image. The transhumanists say that*
*humanity will make itself into God.*

Sebastian Seung

For Kristyna and Vilik
the most amazing humans I have ever met.

# PREFACE

BY LAURENT PHILONENKO

"By 2020, intelligent virtual assistants will do business on behalf of the customer."

I made this prediction in 2001 as a conclusion to the book titled 2020 CRM. The same book also contained some predictions that never materialized, and missed the mark on others. But even back then, we clearly saw the potential for day-to-day applications of Artificial Intelligence (AI).

AI is a major change in and of itself. What does it really change? Simply put, it allows data, and to some extent knowledge, to be processed in order to generate insights or predictions. With traditional tools this would not be possible.

Much has been and continues to be written about AI, but I would reiterate a key notion: a lot of AI applications draw from statistical principles and techniques, and one should keep in mind that by definition, there is no certainty. That the outcome is not as predicted does not mean that the prediction was wrong - this is just the nature of the statistical world. This can lead to rather serious consequences and lead to what is one of the controversies about AI: having the right to understand how a person's data are processed and lead to decisions that can affect individuals profoundly. Techniques such as neural networks are notoriously difficult to debug; if the effect of an error in the model is such that you are routed to the wrong agent, the harm might be minimal. If the error results in a wrong medical treatment or credit assessment, its impact can be more damaging and long lasting.

13

Of course, any writing about AI would be incomplete without mentioning its impact on jobs. There are several schools of thought - some proclaim that massive job destruction is inevitable, while others take a more optimistic tone and conclude that new jobs will emerge, offsetting the losses. The history of technology transitions tends to show that indeed they result in net jobs creation. An interesting thought experiment is to place yourself back in, say, 1900, and think of jobs of today jobs that you could not have possibly imagined back then. There are many, many of them.

Today, AI contributes to advances in fields such as pricing, predictive maintenance, yield optimization in airlines and hotels, fraud and debt analysis, autonomous driving, and customer service, to name just a few. AI is also used in robotics process automation which, as the names indicates, automates repetitive clerical tasks across applications. In each of these fields, the nature of jobs will change. In economic terms, the impact of AI is believed to be enormous: hundreds of billions, even trillions of dollars. This is a tectonic shift.

Customer service stands out as an important category, as it is a highly strategic area for any organization. From companies to government entities, just about everyone wants to retain and upsell to customers or make agencies more productive, provide a better experience, and drive a competitive advantage through service. Customer service representatives, including contact center agents, are the people who interact with customers and often with inadequate tools and systems. It is generally acknowledged that agents represent more than 80% of overall contact centers costs, and for this reason companies have been trying to automate customer interactions for a long time. If the issue can be resolved merely with an interactive voice response (IVR) system, why use an expensive human agent? In some industries, the percentage of calls resolved by IVRs is as high as 80% or more. As new communications modes such as chat and messaging become commonplace in customer service, bots can also help drive the next wave of automation.

There is no doubt that customer service is a fertile ground for AI, for several reasons:

- Customer service is a data-rich environment.
- Contact centers are a highly measured environment, and contact center agents have one of the most metrics-driven professions in the world.
- Millennials and digital natives have high expectations about instant gratification and the expedited resolution of their requests, whether buying a product or getting an issue resolved. When immediacy and relevance are essential, personalization and understanding the customer will save the day. The expectation goes: if I am contacting you, you should know who I am and understand what I want. Therefore, organizations will increasingly require data and models to generate insights and predictions about their customers.

From there, it is easy to assume that AI will be a major factor in customer service. AI will help make sense of all the data and predict the best options for engaging with customers. AI will also analyze customer interactions in real time, whether with structured data such as website clicks or unstructured data such as speech.

Options for customer engagement abound: it used to be by phone only, but now customers can use chat, email, video, messaging, and more - to the extent that what consumers will use five years from now is anyone's guess. Mine is that virtual assistants will play a significant role in helping customers get what they want or need. They will serve as an entry point into companies, making calls or writing messages on behalf of the customer. This does not however mean that the customer will never be involved; for complex transactions or problems, human dialogue, whether by voice or messaging, will still be necessary.

How companies will build and maintain the customer's context, provide interaction modes the customer wants, and anticipate the customer's intent - all the while managing their staff and cost - is really the question. Winners will use the right mix of technology and processes to bring about happiness for their customers as well as job satisfaction and productivity for their customer service representatives.

This is what Vit Horky set out to detail and explain in this book. From a review of what AI means for us and the world to how customer service can evolve, Vit has produced a thought-provoking, facts-filled, aspirational, and concrete guide. Even with my many years in the industry, I have yet to come across another book that combines business, technology, and society considerations in such a lively and interesting way.

It is also remarkable that Vit found the time and energy to write Customer Service in the Transhuman Age while growing a startup, taking care of customers, employees, partners, and investors. This says a lot about the author, who not only sees the big picture from afar but also takes an active part in it. In the book, he lays out a vision for the next years of AI and customer service in a thoughtful and sometimes provocative way. Whether we agree or disagree, Vit makes us think, and while he offers directions, he also invites us to reflect on some of the major trends of our times.

I truly enjoyed this book and hope you will, too.


**Laurent Philonenko**
Laurent Philonenko is a contact center industry leader and visionary. His experience spans nearly 20 years in executive roles serving customers globally, including senior leadership experience at Cisco and Genesys. He is known for melding a deep understanding of customer needs with a unique understanding of technology and trends.

# INTRODUCTION

The phone keeps ringing... For the 15$^{th}$ time today.

The buzzing and vibrating in my pocket instantly increases my heart rate. I don't want to talk to you now, whoever you are! The disturbance caused by somebody dialing my number while I'm trying to focus on work or spending quality time with my family gives me a headache.

It's probably because I was only born 32 years ago and I grew up with internet access and a keyboard at my fingertips, or maybe it's because I find it difficult to multitask. I prefer turning the smartphone display towards my eyes and typing on the screen rather than putting the phone to my ear. And I do it a lot. I'm attached to technology and I keep wondering lately:

How would I feel about throwing my smartphone into the garbage and never answering another call? How would my life change if I never opened an internet browser again? What would I do and where would I go if I couldn't drive a car, fly by plane or travel by train? How would you feel?

We'll soon be celebrating the arrival of the 21$^{st}$ year of the 21$^{st}$ century, and technology plays a larger role in our lives than ever. From the moment you wake up in the morning to the moment you go to sleep at night, if you're living in the developed world, chances are you're in contact with technology just about every minute of the day. And if you use any kind of sleep-monitoring app, you're in touch with technology all night too.

From smartphones to smart homes, FitBits to Facebook and everything in between, technology provides us with huge advantages that would have been unheard of just a few years ago. When your grandparents were young they certainly never imagined that you would be making video calls to friends around the world, or that nearly two billion people would be using an online social network to stay in touch and share photos, thoughts and memories. When you think about it, we're more powerful than ever before, thanks to technology. And we're poised to become even more powerful.

This book argues that the customer service industry will undergo fundamental changes in the upcoming decades due to newly available technologies and evolving consumer behavior. Humans will gain abilities previously associated only with gods, or in other words they will become Transhuman. As a result, companies will need to fundamentally change their approach to customer service in order to develop new revenue opportunities and strengthen market position.

The growing capabilities of Artificial Intelligence, natural language processing and business process automation, and their application to contact centers, will make a large portion of customer service jobs redundant, while increasing the complexity and value of the remaining customer service roles. Since both companies and consumers have embraced recently invented channels like social media, social messaging and mobile apps, these channels will play a major role in customer engagements with brands at the expense of traditional voice channels. Contact center offshoring is expected to decline as contact centers employ more skilled expert agents who will be responsible for complex and empathy-requiring conversations, while simple, frequent inquiries will be fully handled by bots and self-service applications. Businesses will focus more on training, personal development and hiring in-house service agents with broader job responsibilities, leading to higher job satisfaction and lower employee turnover. These changes will have a long-term positive effect on bottom lines but they will require initial and continuous investments into customer service at the expense of other business areas.

As brands continue trying to build long-lasting customer experiences, customer service will take a revenue-generating role within the organization. This will happen through the utilization of deep customer knowledge, along with efficient timing and a focus on the channels of choice, to generate more upsells and cross-sales than today's traditional sales channels.

In the short term, further improvements in the cost efficiency of contact centers will be achieved by the effective use of Intelligent Advisors and other AI-powered technologies, which will fundamentally improve the productivity and quality of customer service jobs. In the long term, brain uploading and scientifically developed telepathic skills, aided by the use of brain chip implants, may contribute to the rapid improvement of knowledge sharing among customer service advisors, while technologies transmitting human thoughts into written text and virtual reality rooms will enable companies to provide a much faster and seamless customer experience without the need for consumers to leave their homes or the comfort of their daily lives.

However, these new technologies also come with great threats to the job market and to the security of human society. Human-level Artificial Intelligence is likely to cause a fundamental disruption of the customer service industry, and companies need to prepare for the growing danger of more advanced customer data theft. The future of more than 14 million customer service workers depends on timely preparation by both businesses, governments and individual customer service professionals.

This book is written for those customer service professionals, as well as for passionate experts and managers across large and small companies. CEOs and managers may get inspired by the numerous use cases and new business opportunities. Customer service, customer experience and IT professionals may put specific use cases into practice through practical checklists and step-by-step guides. Last but not least, this book is written for people like me—those who are both excited and a little scared about how technology will change the world for us and future generations, and who seek to find out what we can do today to unleash the human potential around us.

What you hold in your hands is the result of exciting, sometimes slightly painful, discovery. As you read the next chapters you'll explore the development of transhumanism and how it could improve the way we do customer service in the near future. You'll also find a whole lot of practical advice for moving customer service into the future, starting today. I've tried to make the book as practical as possible, so along with my speculation about what remain unknown possibilities for digital customer service, you'll find plenty of key learnings and step-by-step improvements that I've gathered over nearly a decade in the industry.

I hope you find this book interesting and useful. It's been fun to write and I look forward to many more discussions to come as these technologies continue to develop, along with our understanding of them.

If you're interested in these topics, I'd love to hear from you.

**Vit Horky**
linkedin.com/in/vithorky
vit.horky@brandembassy.com

# 1800s
# GO TO SOURCE

## CUSTOMERS BUYING LOCALLY FROM TRUSTED MERCHANTS

Since the invention of trade thousands of years ago well into the 1800s, humans lived in an era when communication between customers and companies was largely done face to face, or in some cases handled in written letters. What can be considered an offline age from today's perspective was defined by the ability of companies to provide a personal approach and a personal experience for every customer. The relationships between customers and companies were largely built on individual rapport between the customer and the company representative.

The proprietor of a groceries and provisions shop in the UK in the late 1800s.

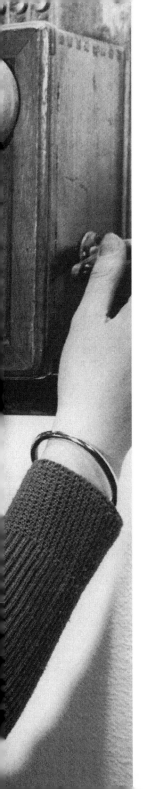

# 1876
# TELEPHONE

## PEOPLE CONNECTING AROUND
## THE WORLD

The invention of the telephone in the
late 19$^{th}$ century and its rapid spread to
the general population during the early
20$^{th}$ century fundamentally changed the
way relationships between brands and
customers were built. The telephone
allowed people around the world to
converse, and for the first time it allowed
direct, immediate connections between
customers and companies who were
separated by great distances. This
was a huge advancement for customer
service, but it also meant that many
customers no longer had personal
relationships with companies.

Woman at telephone from 1905.

# 1960s
# CALL CENTERS

## OFFSHORING CONTACT CENTERS TO CUT COSTS

As the telephone became a necessary accessory for every home and office, it became the preferred method for customer service. However, as volumes increased along with the pressure to cut costs, customer service was usually outsourced to off-shored call centers. This often led to greater efficiency but further increased the distance between customer and company. Meaning that the contact center agent often had little practical knowledge and experience with the products and problems that led customers to get in touch.

Off-shored Business Process Outsourcers (BPOs) employ over 14 million workers in low-cost countries such as India or the Philippines to provide customer service jobs for companies in the developed world. Many BPOs will struggle to maintain a competitive edge as consumers shift from voice to digital channels and expect more skilled customer service advisors.

BPO, Bangalore, Karnataka, India.

# 1970s
# I(VR) ROBOT

## EMPLOYING DEHUMANIZED CUSTOMER SERVICE

The invention of Interactive Voice Response systems (IVR) led to the widespread dehumanization of the interactions between companies and customers. These pre-recorded voice commands made customer service more efficient for companies but also meant that customers could interact with a company on numerous occasions without ever actually speaking to a human being. The personal communication that had dominated customer service for generations was now officially a thing of the past.

The big breakthrough in customer service occurred between the late 1960s and the early 1970s. A new tone dialing methodology and the findings on speech recognition, "The Hidden Markov Model", set the blueprint for IVR.

# 1990s
# INTERNET

### ENGAGING WITH BRANDS FASTER OVER EMAIL AND LIVE CHAT

Thanks to innovators like Bill Gates, the invention and rapid adoption of the internet in the 1990s enabled companies to implement a mass approach to marketing and promotion. They filled email inboxes with bulk emails and covered websites with advertising banners as well as more intelligently targeted advertising campaigns. But the general personalization of content did not advance beyond personal greetings and content alternations for bulk emails, or website content reshuffling based on customer affiliation to a pre-defined customer segment. Email and web-based chat became popular channels for resolving both complex and urgent service issues.

Bill Gates, the founder of Microsoft, helped pioneer personal computers. Microsoft's first retail version of Windows launched in 1985. As personal computers became more popular in the 1990s, the internet developed as an important new communication channel for both personal and corporate use.

Bill Gates working in his office in his younger years.
© Alamy Stock Photo | Photo by Paul Chesley

# 2000s
# SOCIAL MEDIA

## CUSTOMERS GAINING A STRONGER VOICE

With the proliferation of social media in the early 21st century, customers gained a much stronger voice that was capable of influencing companies' policies and behavior. A completely new communication channel opened, one that was more customer-centric and more public than ever before. One disgruntled customer now had the ability to create an international incident and plenty of bad press. At the same time, companies now had an obligation to keep up with more incoming queries and complaints than ever before.

Mark Zuckerberg (L) and Chris Hughes (R) creators of 'Facebook' photographed at Eliot House at Harvard University, Cambridge, MA. on May 14, 2004. Facebook was created in February 2004, 3 months prior to this photograph.

# 2010s
# OMNICHANNEL

## CUSTOMERS GETTING HELP ANY TIME THEY WANT ON THEIR PREFERRED CHANNEL

As more social media channels have caught on and more companies have caught up, customers have come to expect that they can reach a company at any time on any channel. Customers are less patient than ever and companies have to work harder than ever to keep up with requests on a variety of channels. The ability to respond to a customer on any channel with the same quality, often called Omnichannel customer service, has become a necessity for companies trying to maintain a competitive edge. But for companies that have not yet centralized their customer service, this has led to decreased efficiency.

Omnichannel's origins date back to Best Buy's use of customer centricity to compete with Walmart's electronic department in 2003. The company created an approach that centered around the customer both in-store and online, while providing post-sales support.

Project
truction Entry Lev
Mechanical Enginee
legal Part-Time
Payable
Driver Full
keeper Analyst
curity Ins
Representative
state
Au
Medical
eacher Secretary
i
n
urse (RN) Recruiter
vices Representative
er Medical
Analyst Office
l E Cler
n
Pharmacy g
Assistant

# 2020s
# AI DIGITAL CARE

## AUTOMATION ENABLING HUMANS TO FOCUS ON EMPATHY AND COMPLEX ISSUES

With the recent and rapidly developing innovation in Artificial Intelligence, robotics, the Internet of Things, Virtual Reality and Augmented Reality, both customers and company representatives have gained enhanced human abilities that will fundamentally change the way customer service is provided. More companies now employ automation such as chatbots to take care of simple, repetitive customer queries, which frees human agents to focus on more complex issues or ones requiring empathy. The result is improved customer experience, and customer service that's more efficient than ever.

Advancements in technology continue to transform customer service interactions. By 2020, experts project that more than 85% of all customer interactions will be handled without the need for a human agent.

© pixabay

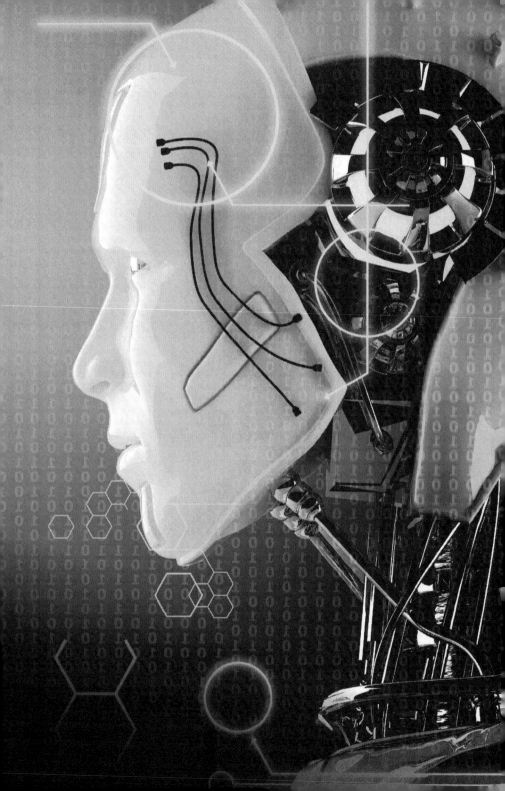

# 2050s
# TRANSHUMAN AGE

## COMPUTERS SURPASSING GENERAL HUMAN INTELLIGENCE

Both customers and customer service agents equipped with systems and applications powered by Artificial Intelligence, coupled with the efficient use of big data and real applications of virtual reality, will change the reasons that customers want or need to interact with customer service departments. It will also revolutionize the way companies leverage automation as a partial replacement of duties traditionally handled by humans, and the way customers and brands develop relationships. Superintelligent computers will be able to solve customer problems in ways that are indistinguishable from human-to-human conversations.

Uploading. Sometimes also called Whole Brain Emulation (WBE), brain uploading or mind copying is the process of scanning the mental state of a particular brain substrate and copying it to a computer. Although today still in a theoretical stage of development, Ray Kurzweil, Director of Engineering at Google, reckons that people will be able to upload their brains and become "digitally immortal" by 2045.

CHAPTER 1

# HOW TRANS- HUMANISM MET CUSTOMER SERVICE

The concept of transhumanism—the idea that someday soon the human body and mind will be augmented with technology that will help us be fitter, happier and more productive—has a long and interesting history stretching back almost to the beginning of the 20th century. This idea may still seem like science fiction to some, but for scientists it's becoming more of a reality every day.

What does transhumanism have to do with customer service? The world of contact centers is not the first thing that would come to mind when discussing transhuman capabilities empowered by super-intelligent computers. However, it's one of many industries that will be, as you will learn in this book, affected by the upcoming growth in Artificial Intelligence and other technologies that may dramatically change the role of humans within the industry as well as the purpose of the customer service industry itself.

This chapter investigates the concept of transhumanism and its history to suggest ways that these developments are going to influence the customer service industry. Although it is unknown how quickly the concepts of transhumanism will materialize in the day-to-day lives of consumers and businesses, companies should pay close attention to transhumanism's development and consider both the opportunities and threats that come with it.

**Customer service is one of many industries that will be affected by the upcoming growth in AI.**

# A BRIEF HISTORY OF TRANSHUMANISM

The human desire to gain god-like abilities is as old as human history. Transhumanism has roots in rational humanism and some of the most prominent Enlightenment thinkers of the 18th century.

> "Man is something that shall be overcome."
> Friedrich Nietzsche

The Age of Enlightenment is often said to have started with the publication of Francis Bacon's Novum Organum, The New Tool,[1] which proposes a scientific methodology based on empirical investigation rather than a priori reasoning. Bacon advocated the project of "effecting all things possible,"[2] by which he meant using science to achieve mastery over nature in order to improve living conditions for human beings. This mode of Renaissance thinking combined with the influence of Isaac Newton, Thomas Hobbes, John Locke, Immanuel Kant, the Marquis de Condorcet and others to form the basis for rational humanism, which emphasized empirical science and critical reason—rather than revelation and religious authority—as ways of learning about the natural world and our place within it.

As we know, Darwin changed everything. After the publication of his book On the Origin of Species (1859),

---

1    Bacon, 1620
2    Bacon, 1620

it became increasingly plausible to view the current version of humanity not as the endpoint of evolution but rather as an early phase in a process that will continue. As we'll see below, this is vital to the concept of transhumanism because it suggests that our cognitive abilities can and will continue to grow under the right circumstances. This was partially what Friedrich Nietzsche had in mind when he created his doctrine of der Übermensch, or "the overman." As he wrote in the 19th century, "I teach you the overman. Man is something that shall be overcome."[3]

Fast forward to 1924, when the noted British biochemist J. B. S. Haldane published the essay "Daedalus; or, Science and the Future," in which he argued that great benefits would come from controlling our own genetics and from science in general.[4] In this important essay, Haldane seems to link Darwin's concept of evolution with his own thinking about the development of genetics, science and technology, which were witnessing phenomenal growth in the early part of the 20th century. In the years since, this growth has only intensified.

In 1957, Julian Huxley, a distinguished biologist who was also the first Director-General of UNESCO and the founder of the World Wildlife Fund, coined the word "transhumanism." In an essay of the same name, Huxley wrote that humans should use any means necessary, including medicine, science and technology, to better themselves and their social and interpersonal environment.[5] This visionary essay laid the groundwork for the rapid development of transhumanism in the coming decades.

3   Nietzsche, 1896
4   Haldane, 1924
5   Huxley, 1957

Another important turning point for transhumanism came in 1965, when Gordon E. Moore, the co-founder of Intel, noticed that the number of transistors on a chip exhibited exponential growth. This led to the formulation of "Moore's Law," which states (roughly) that computing power doubles every 18 months to two years.[6] More recently, Ray Kurzweil has documented similar exponential growth rates in a number of other technologies.[7] It is interesting to note that the world economy, a general index of humanity's productive capacity, has doubled about every 15 years in modern times.

> **"Within thirty years, we will have the technological means to create superhuman intelligence. Shortly after, the human era will be ended."**
> Vernor Vinge

Even more recently, science fiction author and professor Vernor Vinge has written about the concept of "Technological Singularity,"[8] stating that "within thirty years, we will have the technological means to create superhuman intelligence. Shortly after, the human era will be ended." Transhumanists today hold diverging views about this idea. Some see it as a likely scenario, while others believe that it is more probable that there will never be any very sudden and dramatic changes as a result of progress in Artificial Intelligence.

Whether you believe that humans will soon achieve god-like capabilities of learning and cognition depends on how much faith you have in technology. But there is

6   Moore, 1965
7   Baer, 2015
8   Vinge, 1993

something universally human about the quest for advancing knowledge and ability. Let's take a closer look at my own.

# THE HUMAN RACE FOR HIGHER INTELLIGENCE

**If everyone were more intelligent, wouldn't the world be a better place?**

When I was a kid I used to think I had superpowers. Blasting a bunch of bad guys from another planet (impersonated by kindergarten enemies) back to space with a laser beam shot from my arms? No prob. Jumping from a burning five-story building and landing softly with a scared poodle puppy to the amazement of some good-looking lady standing nearby? Easy. Pushing my fist through the wall of our grammar school classroom to blow off some steam after I got a "C" on my math test? Piece of cake. Gradually, I learned that I hadn't inherited any powers that my pals Superman, Batman and Spider Man would consider cool. But as my wife says, I realized that "just a little later" in life than I should have.

The next step in my mission to find my place on earth was the belief that I had Superintelligence. I had finally figured it out: My brain was my superpower! "I am more capable of coming up with world-saving inventions than anybody else," I thought. Inventing the next big thing required proper preparation, so I patiently read biographies of the world's smartest people: Nikola Tesla, Albert Einstein, Thomas A. Edison, Daniel Kahneman, Steve Jobs and others. I realized that the best, most impactful inventions in the world (like penicillin, pesticide, electricity, and the internet) were made by highly intelligent people. If everyone were more intelligent, wouldn't the world be a better place? What if all humans had super-powerful brains? The good news is we're getting there, slowly but surely. Because we are getting smarter.

# THE EVOLUTION OF INTELLIGENCE

Would you have the same intelligence if you had been born 100 years earlier? Most likely. Had you been born to a well-educated, well-off family, you would probably be able to read books by the age of 10, write love letters to your sweetheart by 15 and calculate your finances by the time you started your first job. You brain would measure approximately 1,300 cm$^3$.[9] No fundamental change compared to today's "you."

But if you were born two million years ago, how intelligent would you be? Well, that's a whole different story. As a member of the Homo Habilis family living between 2.1 and 1.8 million years ago, your brain would have been

---

9    Ordy, 1975

about 600 cm³.[10] You'd have a large face, tiny canines and massive chewing teeth (which earned you and your friends the nickname of "the Nutcracker man").[11] You'd only be 1.3-meters tall, which means you're larger than many other animals, but embarrassingly small in 21st century terms. As a Homo Habilis you'd also have a rather limited intelligence, with the ability to use basic tools for scavenging but not much more than that.

The size and structure of your brain matters. Species with larger brains tend to have higher intelligence.[12] This doesn't mean that you can consider yourself smarter than your friend because your head is bigger, but when you compare the brain weight of all living species on the planet, humans come out on top, only beaten by whales and elephants which, although smart, do not have the intelligence of humans. However, brain size and weight alone are not the most important thing. It's the ratio between the weight of the brain and the overall weight of the species that most clearly shows that humans are intellectually superior to other living species.[13] That's why ants can't calculate their household finances (although they can embarrass any human by lifting three times their weight). Humans are far more intelligent than any other creature on the planet because their brain is large and their brain structure is very complex. Moreover, no general difference in intelligence between men and women has been scientifically proven although men are said to have slightly larger brains (as their entire body and skull is bigger

10   Pickrell, 2006
11   Wood, 2014
12   Botkin-Kowacki, 2016
13   Botkin-Kowacki, 2016

too). Women, on the contrary, have more structured brains, so they can do more with less.[14] What's clear is that human intelligence has increased over time and the humans of today are fundamentally more intelligent than our ancestors.

> **Human intelligence has increased over time and the humans of today are fundamentally more intelligent than our ancestors.**

Intelligent species are less likely to eat poisonous food and water, or walk off a cliff. Intelligent people are also more likely to get an education, find a job and receive a decent salary. Plus, intelligent people are more likely to find a sexual partner, then reproduce and create more intelligent offspring. Being intelligent matters. We can also argue that intelligent people are more likely to come up with new inventions and societal improvements. Intelligence is good, and the more you have the better.

# WILL OUR INTELLIGENCE CONTINUE TO INCREASE?

In the late 20th century the scientist James R. Flynn found that human intelligence roughly increases by three IQ points every 10 years. This might be because humans increasingly work with abstract models rather than shovels,

14   Halpern, et. al., 2014

and genetics might be in play too. That's great! So if you want to be more intelligent, tell your mom to wait a bit longer before bringing you into the world... or maybe not. Recently some experts have pointed out that we might see the end of the Flynn Effect in developed countries and the general IQ might actually start to decrease over time. Some scientists, including Flynn himself, claim that this trend might be reversed through better education. As Michio Kaku, a theoretical physicist, points out,[15] formal teaching in the future will focus on conceptual thinking and principles, as the need for memorization will completely vanish with the popularization of internet-connected contact lenses that can seamlessly access a vast array of basic information when the pupil blinks his or her eyes.

Human intelligence is now extremely developed, as larger-headed babies are more difficult to give birth to and large brains are demanding in terms of oxygen and nutrient requirements.[16] The size of the human skull hasn't changed much in recent centuries. We might be hitting the limits of what nature can do with our heads.[17] That leads us to an important question: how can we continue the historic process of increasing human intelligence despite the physical limitations? For those who believe this journey is worth exploring, there are a few options out there. One of them includes "outsourcing" human intelligence to a computer.

15   Maritz, 2017
16   Nilsson, 1996
17   Nilsson, 1996

50

# OUTSOURCING INTELLIGENCE TO COMPUTERS

Unlike the human head, computers can be as large as we want. Many, like IBM's "Blue Gene," exceed the size of a typical one--bedroom apartment. A room-size IBM System/370 computer in the 1970s was smart enough for complex calculations, but dumb enough to make mistakes if not precisely monitored.[18]

While today's computers have a vastly higher IQ than humans when it comes to repetitive tasks or deep learning, humans still outperform computers in many ways. According to Murray Shanahan, Professor of Cognitive Robotics for the Department of Computing at Imperial College London, "Computers can outperform humans on certain specialized tasks, such as playing [the game] Go or chess, but no computer program today can match a human's general intelligence. Humans learn to achieve many different types of goals in a huge variety of environments. We don't yet know how to endow computers with the kind of common sense understanding of the everyday world that underpins human general intelligence, although I'm sure we will succeed in doing this one day."[19]

How smart are the smartest computers in the second half of the second decade of the 21st century? AlphaZero, the game-playing AI created by Google's sibling DeepMind, is

---

18   System/370 Announcement, 1970
19   Whitney, 2017

a good example. This repurposed AI, which has repeatedly beaten the world's best Go players as AlphaGo, has been generalized so that it can now learn other games. It took just four hours to learn the rules to chess before beating the world champion chess program, Stockfish 8, in a 100-game match up.[20] And while this computer took only four hours to learn chess, it took almost a decade for IBM's Deep Blue computer to learn the game well enough to beat Gary Kasparov in 1997. The speed at which computers learn and gain abilities is growing exponentially.[21]

# BEYOND HUMAN INTELLIGENCE

Who's the smartest person you can think of? Stephen Hawking, Nikola Tesla, Albert Einstein, or maybe your dad? For Nick Bostrom, Director of the Future of Humanity Institute and the Governance of Artificial Intelligence Program at Oxford University (and one of the smartest people I can think of), it's Edward Witten, the theoretical physician and co-author of String Theory.[22] Now, what's the intellectual distance between the smartest person you know and the village idiot? For many, comparing their intellects would be like comparing apples and oranges.

20  Gibbs, 2017
21  Higgins, 2017
22  Bostrom, 2015

But the intellectual distance between the two would look something like this:

Village Idiot                                    Ed Witten

Bostrom 2018

For a computer equipped with Artificial Intelligence, reaching the intelligence of the village idiot is actually quite difficult. In fact it probably still hasn't happened. Although some computer technologies drive autonomous cars, are capable of beating Gary Kasparov in chess, or can calculate the exact flight trajectory of a reusable rocket, these technologies will outsmart a human being only in one specific discipline. Emotional Intelligence (EQ)–the ability to understand other humans on an emotional level and use appropriate emotions in personal interactions–is what computers are missing. And that's why it's difficult for computers to replace humans in activities that even a four--year old could master. Try to make a computer compose a fairytale and you won't get a very happy ending!

# WILL AI FAIL TO BE REALIZED?

Current technologies remain limited, but that doesn't mean we haven't made immense progress in the development of AI. Back in the 1970s and 1980s, several scientists and members of the media had high hopes for reaching human--level Artificial Intelligence in just a few years. They have been proven wrong and much of the early progress in Artificial Intelligence has stagnated as a result. Now we realize that computers back then were not nearly as powerful as they needed to be to match the intelligence of humans. Approximately 75 to 100 Teraops, or Trillions of Operations Per Second, are required for human-like performance.[23]

Back in the '70s, computers were capable of reaching the intelligence of an insect. The computers that are currently in development are not far from reaching the capacities required to match human intelligence. For general AI technology, which is capable of demonstrating the same variety of skills as a human being, reaching human intelligence is not far away. Given the fact that AI capabilities are growing exponentially, it is possible that a computer could reach the intelligence of a mouse, then a chimp and quickly after that the intelligence of the village idiot, achieving the admirable levels of Albert Einstein or Ed Witten and then continuing ever more quickly to an unimaginable intelligence that far exceeds the human brain.

23   Bostrom, 1997. Some neuroscientists suggest this is perhaps an overestimate.

The intellectual distance for AI looks like this:

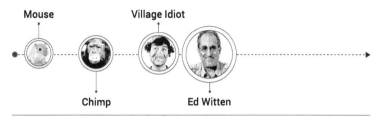

Bostrom, 2015

> "Machine intelligence is the last invention that humanity will ever need to make."
> Nick Bostrom

For several decades, the computing power found in advanced Artificial Intelligence and robotics systems has been stuck at the insect brain power of 1 Million Instructions Per Second (MIPS). While computer power per dollar has risen rapidly, the money available has fallen just as fast. The earliest days of AI, in the mid 1960s, were fuelled by lavish post-Sputnik defense funding, which gave researchers access to $10,000,000 (~€8,600,000) supercomputers. In the post--Vietnam war days of the 1970s, funding declined, and only $1,000,000 (~€860,000) machines were available. By the early 1980s, AI research had to settle for $100,000 (~€86,000) minicomputers. In the late 1980s, the available machines were $10,000 (~€8,600) workstations. By the 1990s, a great deal of work was being done on personal computers that cost only a few thousand dollars. Since then, AI and robot brain power have improved, along with the efficiency of computers. By 1993 personal computers provided 10 MIPS, by 1995 it was 30 MIPS, and in 1997 it was over 100 MIPS. Now, suddenly machines are reading text and recognizing speech, and robots are driving themselves cross-country.[24] Computer capabilities have rapidly increased over the past decades and that creates exciting new possibilities for the use of Artificial Intelligence.

As Bostrom points out, once AI reaches human-level intelligence, it will consistently improve its capabilities thanks to a continuous feedback loop. AI will help construct better AI and the new AI will help invent even better AI, and so on. Even if no advancement in software development is achieved, the AI would be able to think twice as fast as a human being once hardware is upgraded with doubled processing power. We would soon have computers with so-called "weak superintelligence"[25] possessing the capabilities of the human brain but thinking twice as fast as humans. Imagine what Albert Einstein or Stephen Hawking could have invented with twice as much time in their lives! But it must be admitted that some critics of Bostrom think he is too optimistic in his estimates about the time it will take for AI to reach such levels. We'll see.

Critics and AI enthusiasts agree that Artificial Intelligence creates opportunities in two ways: Helping human workers move into more meaningful jobs and assisting human workers with computational support in their daily tasks. This makes them more efficient and perhaps even makes their jobs more enjoyable. In the customer service industry specifically,

24  Moravec, 1997
25  Bostrom, 1997

computers are increasingly able to automatically resolve many customer inquiries. Meanwhile for the many complex conversations that require empathy there are human customer service agents supported by AI-powered Intelligent Advisors that suggest appropriate responses or guide the agents to relevant knowledge sources. As computers become better at understanding customer intent and making appropriate judgements and autonomous decisions, they will help to automate more of the activities currently handled by humans.

Many consider this rapid advancement of AI capabilities scary. How can computers rule the world without understanding human values? How can a piece of metal decide whether an autonomous car will crash into a pedestrian or kill the driver instead by trying to avoid the collision? How can humans trust their lives to something that's not human? We should all ask these and many more questions as we develop our understanding of the threats and opportunities of AI's advancements. Just consider this: What's the software on your personal computer you trust most?

## How can humans trust their lives to something that's not human?

You've probably placed your trust in some antivirus software that has access to critical parts of your computer's functionality and your personal data. Am I right? Now imagine this antivirus software actually contained a superintelligent virus that kept learning your behavioral patterns and your personal data and storing everything without using it for many years. And then, one day, one absolutely usual day for you, it takes everything it knows and uses it to drain your saving accounts, sell your personal health data to the highest bidder, and blackmail you with all the computer content you never want others to see. Then it reaches out to your friends on your behalf to suggest downloading "this absolutely amazing antivirus software that has saved me tons of headaches." Something that you trusted completely could ruin your life in a way you failed to imagine because your intelligence is actually lower than that of the computer that now controls your life. That's Superintelligence gone wrong, and a lot of work still needs to be done to avoid these situations. Later chapters will explore laws, regulations and other ways to minimize the risks of AI breaking bad.

For now, let's get back to the village idiot. For him, reaching the intelligence of Albert Einstein is unthinkable. For Albert Einstein, doubling his intelligence was, most likely, also unthinkable. But what you learned in this chapter means that it's just one evolutionary step for AI to double human intelligence. And it's a step that AI will take before making another series of bigger and bigger steps. And it's beyond the intelligence of your author to understand what this will mean for society! By the way, have you ever tried to think about what brains 100 times or 1,000 times smarter than a human's could accomplish? It's hard to come up with anything really astonishing, right? That's because compared to these brains we are simply too stupid to imagine it, and there is no smarter organism on this planet that can tell us.

**Trying to outsmart something 1,000 times smarter than us is pointless.**

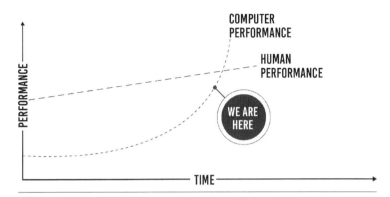

Graph by Jeremy Howard from his TED talk "The Wonderful and Terrifying Implications of Computers that Can Learn.", Howard, 2014

# HUMAN-LEVEL AI
# BY 2040?

If you're excited about Superintelligence, you might be wondering when we're actually going to see it. In 2013, Vincent C. Müller and Nick Bostrom conducted a survey that asked hundreds of AI experts the following: "For the purposes of this question, assume that human scientific activity continues without major negative disruption. By what year would you see a (10% / 50% / 90%) probability for such Human-Level Machine Intelligence [or what we call AGI[26]] to exist?"[27] The survey "asked them to name an optimistic

26  AGI stands for Artificial General Intelligence
27  Urban, 2015

year (one in which they believe there's a 10% chance we'll have AGI), a realistic guess (a year they believe there's a 50% chance of AGI — i.e. after that year they think it's more likely than not that we'll have AGI), and a safe guess (the earliest year by which they can say with 90% certainty we'll have AGI)."[28] These are the summarized results:

**Median optimistic year (10% likelihood) → 2022**
**Median realistic year (50% likelihood) → 2040**
**Median pessimistic year (90% likelihood) → 2075**

The median participant thinks it's more likely than not that we'll have computers with human-level intelligence in 20 years. It's unknown what will happen once computers are smarter than humans. Some scientists argue that the methodology of the survey favored those experts who are more optimistic about the prospects of Superintelligence, but whatever the truth, we will most likely find out within two generations. Your granddaughters might face a very different education system, job market, and living conditions than you experience today.

28  Urban, 2015

# MEET THE TRANSHUMAN CUSTOMER SERVICE AGENT

You're probably wondering how all of this connects to customer service. While there will be some huge revolutions in technology in the future and these will certainly affect the way we do customer service, it's important to recognize that customer service has changed considerably in recent decades, thanks to technological advancement. When I recently entered the contact center at a Fortune 500 communications company in Europe, I was amazed by the friendly and dynamic working environment full of positive people of various ages and ethnicities. Moreover, they were using some of the most advanced technologies available on the market. Complex incoming customer requests, never before encountered by other customer service agents, were handled with the help of intelligent knowledge bases that suggested an optimal response.

Only seconds after incoming customer messages and emails were received by the company's cloud-based servers, automated semantic and sentiment analysis appropriately judged the topic of the conversation, the concerned products and services, the seriousness of the issue, its urgency, and to what extent the customer was upset. By processing all this in real-time, a software selected the customer service agent with the most appropriate skill set to respond to the person in need.

The customer service reps in this company have gained specific expert knowledge so each small team of agents can handle uniquely complex problems without having to call technical engineers or depend on long technical manuals.

Some of the expert reps were equipped with access to social media so they could respond to thousands of customers by sending a single proactive message on Twitter or Facebook. Although the company receives thousands of customer complaints and bug reports every day, the contact center, with over 500 agents, has managed to maintain high productivity, very low employee turnover and a friendly company culture.

If today's customer service agents can do all that, what could a transhuman customer service agent do? Imagine a customer service agent sitting behind a desk in a contact center, looking like any other person you know. You approach and see a woman in her 40s sitting comfortably in a modern seat in front of a large horizontal LCD screen that covers the entire office desk. The touch display looks kind of lonely, you realize, without its usual friends—a keyboard, mouse, or a PC itself. The woman wears a simple black headband that neatly covers part of her head. The wireless headband looks like a piece of avant-garde fashion, but then you see that all her colleagues are wearing one.

You take another step, and you're close enough to touch her shoulder, but she doesn't react. She just sits there without moving. Is she sleeping? Or reading whatever is on the computer display? You look at the display and see a large photo of a customer surrounded by more customer details on one side. Most of the display is covered by bubbles of text conversation exchanged between the customer and the headband-wearing woman. Then the display starts doing something weird—it opens a video file and plays a fast--forwarded recording of someone trying to fix a mobile phone with their bare hands. The camera is pointing at objects like it is attached to the head of the person. Then the video stops and you see another bubble pop up. Now it seems like a customer service agent is typing a message. But it's too fast!

The words appear onscreen faster than even the most masterful typist could manage. You stand there confused. There's a customer service agent sitting in front of you, motionless but apparently busy doing something with a display that seems to be disconnected from any accessory that enables a computer to be used, but the customer on the other end of the line is clearly being helped and consequently after less than a minute the conversation is concluded and the satisfied customer adds a five-star rating. Then the bubbles disappear for a few moments before a new customer photo and conversation pops up.

You have just witnessed my vision of a customer service conversation in the not too distant future. Customer service agents will be equipped with multisensory chips attached to their heads. These chips will transmit signals into the brain, allowing the agents to read incoming information and respond to it at the speed of thought rather than by talking or typing. The agent's eyes will be equipped with removable contact lenses that enable him or her to record or play video by using their eyes as cameras and their brain as the hard drive. The lenses will display additional information to the agent that cannot be effectively displayed on computer screens.

Some transhuman customer service agents will use mind-reading abilities, enabling them to experience an event through the eyes of the customer. Some will have a brain chip implant connected to an online knowledge base, enabling an in-store agent to use the collective wisdom of all agents in real-time while responding to a customer. They'll also be able to read the customer's true emotions by looking at their face or listening to their voice, enabling the agent to use the right techniques to improve the customer's emotional state. These transhuman professionals will use their black wireless headbands to type a computer response 100x faster using the speed of thought rather than their fingers. And at the end of their work shift they'll upload everything they have learned, including past customer resolution experiences, to a collective knowledge base for further use by any other agent. They'll do this simply by confirming a computer command and using their chip implant or removable headband to transmit part of their brain content to secured cloud-based storage.

In the near future we will most likely be able to bring some or all of the transhuman capabilities mentioned above (and many others duly ignored by the author) into the contact center to unleash the potential of humans on a much larger scale. As human intelligence has increased over time, so has the intelligence of the technology we use. It is only a matter of time before AI can augment human capabilities while vastly surpassing the human intellect. It's only logical that customer service keep up with these advances. In the next chapter, we'll look more closely at how customers have changed their behavior, what technologies they use and the ways transhumanism can affect and improve their lives. We'll also look at some of the risks and threats technological advancement may bring too.

# CHAPTER SUMMARY

Humans have tried to gain superpowers since the beginning of time. Recently, scientists have focused their attention on computer-powered human augmentation by Artificial Intelligence. AI helps human workers be more productive. Although we don't know when computers will attain the intelligence of humans, it will likely happen within the next 60 years, and some say as soon as 2040. Customer service is one of many industries that will be significantly affected by the upcoming growth in Artificial Intelligence capabilities. Companies should pay close attention to its development and consider both the opportunities and threats it brings.

# CHAPTER 2

# THE
# CUSTOMER
# IN CHARGE

Chapter 1 introduced the concept of Transhumanism, highlighting some of the ways customer service is already influenced by advanced technology, and how it will do so even more in the future. In this chapter I'd like to look more closely at how upcoming technological developments will change the way customer service agents work, and how most of these changes are driven by the customers.

# YOU IN 1890 COMPARED TO YOU TODAY

Imagine waking up in dirty sheets on a wooden bed along with 10 other people in a hostel on the Upper East Side of Manhattan in 1890. Horse-drawn carriages criss-cross the street four floors down. People are hurrying to work and trying not to get hit, all the while dodging thousands of piles of horse excrement on the muddy streets, none of which have sidewalks. The telephone, the most advanced means of communication in existence, has recently been invented, though it's only available to the privileged few. Most of the streets and all the households are dark from dusk to sunrise since electric streetlights are still a few years off.

When your shoe gets a hole in it, you go to a local cobbler. When you need to discuss a financial loan for your business, you go to a local bank. When you need to get something delivered from far away, you send a letter and get a response a few weeks later. Every Sunday you go to church. And let's say one day you miraculously go on a time-traveling journey to the year 2018. What would you see?

You might step into a cafe and see someone talking with friends in Australia, England and Romania at the same time via something called Skype. No letters, no carrier pigeons and no waiting weeks or even months for a response. What you're seeing is instant communication across the world. And having connections throughout the world is useful in this future, because even students who barely make any money are able to travel around the world on low-fare airlines.

Looking around the cafe a bit more you'd see there's a very popular website called Facebook where more than two billion people share their life stories. That's more than the population of the world in 1890![29] At the same time, you'd see that those people on their computers have access to all of human knowledge from the beginning of time through something called Google.

If you happened to go into a hospital, you'd see doctors transplanting hearts and making prosthetic limbs that can be moved by the power of thought. No more bone saws and wooden crutches! And that new medical technology would be useful, because you'd also see people older than 90 walking the streets and driving electric cars. You'd see dozens of children born and living healthy lives. You'd be amazed because your life expectancy is only 42.5 years in the US in the late 19th century, when one in five infants didn't survive their first month.[30]

If you time traveled from 1890 to 2018 you'd see all this and think: "Wow. These people know everything and

29  Roser and Ortiz-Ospina, 2017
30  "Life Expectancy by Age, 1850–2011"

everyone, they live long, and they can travel anywhere. These people are not humans like us. They are more. These people have powers only associated with gods. In other words, they're transhuman."

Today's technology and science have given us many aspects of life that would be considered beyond-human from a historic perspective. In customer service specifically, companies both large and small have access to technologies that allow them to deliver a high level of personalized, results-driven customer service at mass scale, at costs available to even tightly budgeted businesses.

# THE TRANSHUMAN IN ALL OF US

You, me, and the average digital consumer are already transhuman in many ways (despite not knowing it).

Internet-connected consumers have instant access to the world's collective wisdom through **search engines**, big data processing and peer-to-peer services. They have the ability to connect to the entire collective wisdom of humanity simply by opening up an internet browser. So when customers get in touch with a company these days, they often know a whole lot about that company, its products and services, and how it compares with the competition. That calls for a new approach to customer service. But there's more to digital customer service than smarter customers. Today's digital customers have another advantage that customers in the past never had: an individual voice that's capable of causing fundamental brand damage because of sharing on **social media**, as well as vlogging and blogging. Customer experience is more important than ever because bad customer service has a way of going viral. These days companies are never dealing with only one customer, because every experience that a customer has with a company is likely to be shared widely across digital channels, often to the detriment of the company. Customers have more power than ever.

> **Internet-connected consumers have the ability to connect to the entire collective wisdom of humanity simply by opening up an internet browser. That calls for a new approach to customer service.**

But it's also important to realize how communication has changed from the point of view of the company. Every company now has the ability to speak to thousands of customers in a tailored manner through automated content **personalization** like mass emails. It has never been easier for companies to reach large numbers of customers instantly and in a personalized way. At the same time, companies have gained in-depth knowledge about their consumers and their behavior in real-time through massive customer data collection and **big data** analytics. Companies have more powerful tools than were previously imaginable to help them learn about their customers. Plus, customer service agents have gained access to detailed business and personal data about their customers. This can be used for delivering personal customer experience at scale by companies both large and small.

Companies these days also have the ability to automate large portions of the customer service interactions that were traditionally handled by humans, through the use of AI-powered **chatbots** and virtual assistants. What's more, customer service agents can provide more complex and in-depth support without lengthy education and training processes, thanks to the efficient usage of AI-powered **intelligent assistants** (IA) and other systems that use Natural Language Processing (NLP) and neural networks to access knowledge bases containing thousands of previously resolved customer inquiries.

Many customer service issues will soon be resolved proactively before the customer notices anything, as companies leverage the potential of the **Internet of Things** (IoT) — products sending error reports from a distance and receiving automated software patches or getting hardware components delivered. In the near future, the consumer won't need to visit the customer service department, as both consumers and companies will benefit from the utilization of **Virtual Reality** (VR) and **Augmented Reality** (AR), enabling the simulation of product issues or the resolution of such issues at a distance in virtual service rooms.

We tend to take these developments for granted, but in fact if you take a step back, it's easy to see just how far we've come. Both customers and companies have gained abilities that would have seemed superhuman just a few generations ago. However, the customer service industry is not quite there yet when it comes to leveraging what's already available on the market. So now it's time to visit the contact center of today.

> Both customers and companies have gained abilities that would have seemed superhuman just a few generations ago.

# TRADITIONAL CALL CENTERS ARE DECLINING

Have you ever heard a friend say something like this: "I had this problem with my [add any gadget you use every day], so I called customer service and they were amazing and solved everything so quickly..." No? Let's try another one: "My iPhone stopped working so I called the damn operator, then waited on hold for five minutes while listening to that stupid Lady Gaga song only to be connected to an agent who redirected me to another agent because he had no clue what I was talking about..." Getting closer? Now how about this one: "My phone stopped working, it's so frustrating... It totally messed up my week! It made me realize how much I depend on my smartphone. Can you take a look at what's wrong with it? Contacting customer service is literally the last thing I want to do..."

Sound familiar? Consumers today will do anything to avoid contacting customer service. They'll ask friends or colleagues, Google it, or use self-service portals. This might sound great from the company's perspective, as self-service deflects calls, saving money and allowing the company to focus on customer acquisition and up-sells. But the reality is that by avoiding personal conversations, companies miss the chance to build customer relationships.

Tony Hsieh, CEO of Zappos, sums up the new reality of customer service nicely: "We actually want to talk to our customers. We found that if we get the interaction right, customers remember that for a very long time. We don't have scripts and we don't measure call time in the name of efficiency. We just try to provide that really human connection."[31]

We're not talking about a total technological change, but a complete behavioral shift as consumers own the most powerful phones in history while making fewer calls than ever. The truth is that people have realized that making a phone call is not the best way to resolve their issues while they're waiting for their cappuccino at the local coffee shop, chatting with their colleagues in a meeting room, or strolling the streets of New York City with their newborn sleeping in the stroller.

> **Consumers own the most powerful phones in history while making fewer calls than ever.**

But these technological advancements haven't been reflected in many contact centers. Consider this observation from journalist Aurelio A. Pena, of one of the Philippines' largest call center firms after a graveyard shift that starts at 10 pm and ends at 6 am: "Like zombies, they stumbled out of the elevator: haggard, red-eyed, and sleepy in shabby, crumpled clothes and disheveled hair. Some in sandals and pajamas, their hands gripping either a big coffee mug or a water bottle, they chatter away in English."[32]

31   Hsieh, 2013
32   Pena, 2008

Let's take a moment to consider what some, rather under-developed, call centers look like. As of today, if you contact the call center of any of Fortune 500 company, you'll probably reach a friendly representative with a slight accent (if they don't fool you, as many of them have gone through speech training to sound like Londoners or New Yorkers). Let's call him Aaran.

Most likely, Aaran picked up the phone or got to your live chat message over 6,000 miles and 10 time zones away from you, in the city of New Delhi. He's never used any product or service you've used, he's never been to your country and his knowledge about your situation, environment, and emotional state is absolutely foreign to him. That's not his fault. He earns 245,000 Indian Rupee annually, or about $3,500 (€3,000),[33] which equals what an average skilled cashier in a retail store in the US would make in just two months.[34] Plus, Aaran probably won't be picking up your message six months from now, as the employee turnover in offshore call centers often reaches 80% annually,[35] which means that eight out of 10 agents will soon be working elsewhere. But don't worry, there are another 3,000 of Aaran's colleagues sitting in the same open-space office ready to pick up where he left off. They've all been trained in a similar fashion, all of them have very limited experience (if any) of using the products and services you will be calling about next week, and they all have the same lackluster salary and career prospects.

33   Customer Service Representative Salaries in India," 2018
34   "Payscale," 2017
35   Bool, Sale, 2009

I don't want to sound alarmist, but this is the current picture of a traditional off-shored call center. This is who's responsible for improving the experience and influencing the loyalty of today's knowledgeable, experienced, increasingly educated customers who are connected to 500+ Facebook friends at any moment, and using augmented-reality-powered Pokémon GO apps on iPhones that have more operational memory than the PC Aaran has on his desk.

The fact is, traditional call centers as described above are about to die. Change is inevitable, as call centers have become irrelevant to most of today's customers. But as traditional call centers gradually disappear, they will be replaced by something more dynamic and technologically advanced.

# THE RISE OF DIGITAL

Contact center interactions are expected to increase not just in volume, but also in complexity over the next two years.[36] And the content of incoming queries isn't the only thing that's becoming more complex. The channels that customers use are also changing, and their variety is increasing.

Who would have thought, 10 years ago, that some social messaging app called WhatsApp would soon connect over one billion users with brands, or that Facebook and Twitter would account for around 5% of all contact center interactions? But it's true. Contacts by phone are expected

36  Deloitte, 2017

to fall from 64% of interactions today to 47% in 2019.[37] You read that right: in less than two years, fewer than half of customers will be using their phones for customer service.

Although the demise of the telephone for customer service has long been forecast, most of the migration from phone is expected to go toward chat and social media, along with video chat and co-browsing. Customer service interactions on video chat are forecast to double by 2019.[38] During that time, social media will likely emerge as a mainstream medium for customer service. It's expected to expand from just 4% of contact center interactions today to 9% in 2019.[39]

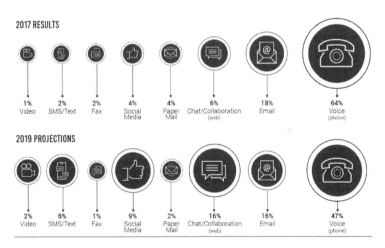

2017 RESULTS

| 1% | 2% | 2% | 4% | 4% | 6% | 18% | 64% |
|---|---|---|---|---|---|---|---|
| Video | SMS/Text | Fax | Social Media | Paper Mail | Chat/Collaboration (web) | Email | Voice (phone) |

2019 PROJECTIONS

| 2% | 6% | 1% | 9% | 2% | 16% | 16% | 47% |
|---|---|---|---|---|---|---|---|
| Video | SMS/Text | Fax | Social Media | Paper Mail | Chat/Collaboration (web) | Email | Voice (phone) |

Global Contact Center Survey, Deloitte, 2017

37   Deloitte, 2017
38   Deloitte, 2017
39   Deloitte, 2017

Will offshore call centers prevail after the shift to digital? Probably not. As you might have guessed when reading about the call centers in the Philippines or India, the gap between the current state of offshore sites and the near-future needs of consumers is just too wide. Moreover, salaries in developing countries are gradually increasing and at the same time, as you will learn in the following chapters, basic tasks can be increasingly handled by computers, so the benefits of offshoring customer service is diminished. Some senior executives of large enterprises have already recognized that, and 20% of them are currently looking to expand their in-house staff by 2019.[40] Also, we see a growing trend of hiring more skilled agents, investing into the recruitment of specialized talents, expanding training programs and increasing salaries.

Most of the Fortune 500 and Global 2000 telecommunication, banking and retail agents assigned to respond to social media and messaging customer requests are in-house, typically based in rural contact centers within the targeted market. This may be a growing trend in the upcoming years, although there is no recent research that proves it, and a number of off-shored contact centers are currently working to modernize their facilities and technologies as well as processes and trainings to avoid being the first to see their contracts cut.

40  Deloitte, 2017

# HOW ARE CONSUMER EXPECTATIONS CHANGING?

As consumers shift from voice to digital channels, companies need to protect and grow revenues traditionally generated through up-sells and cross-sales in the call center. At the same time, as customers increasingly rely on digital channels for customer service, they expect fast, personalized responses across a variety of channels. This necessitates a paradigm shift in the way companies think about customer service and the way they communicate with their customers.

## PERSONALIZED AND IMMEDIATE

These days, companies are expected to respond in real-time, and provide personalized omnichannel experience as consumers become increasingly impatient and have higher expectations and more knowledge.

Picture this: Luisa, our exemplary hypothetical customer, was 20 years old when Mark Zuckerberg launched Facebook in 2004. She recently turned 34. She lives in sunny San Diego, California and owns a Ford SUV. She shops online at least once a week, spends over 3.5 hours online daily[41] via her iPhone, and an additional one hour online via her

41   Statistica, 2017

personal computer[42] every day. In fact, she touches her phone over 2,400 times a day, and like eight out of 10 of all American citizens,[43] she is an active Facebook user who spends an hour a day[44] scrolling through her wall and posting pictures and status updates to her friends. She is educated, with five years of professional experience, she has traveled to three continents and is very sociable with her friends and family, who are always just a few clicks away. Quite possibly, she is also married to an employed, economically active husband and has a small baby boy and a mortgage for their two-bedroom apartment.

Recently, Luisa's wifi stopped working while she was shopping online for new shoes at Nordstrom. And it happened just as she was searching for reviews of the newest Nikes. Damn! Not comfortable picking one of the many models without knowing whether they are good for running her five-mile routine every other morning at Balboa Park, and not really trusting the staff at her local Nordstrom, Luisa desperately needs to get back online. She goes to the nearby Starbucks, connects to wifi, opens her Facebook app, looks up the AT&T page and initiates a Messenger conversation asking to top up her data package, hoping to avoid an annoying wait on their always-busy toll-free hotline, and not wanting to send an email to get a response after the weekend.

Luisa expects to get a response in a few minutes. She also expects that the agent who responds won't ask her about any details she can't remember (**Sharing my phone number is fine, but don't ask for my customer ID**

42  Statistica, 2017
43  Statistica, 2017
44  Stewart, 2016

**or communication password!).** And she expects that her problem will be resolved instantly on Facebook Messenger **(You'd better not tell me that somebody needs to call me back!).** Finally, she assumes that she'll receive informal, friendly support that's similar to what she would expect from the running mates she communicates with on Messenger at the same time **(I'm done with you, AT&T, if you call me "Dear Customer" one more time!).**

Luisa is your average social and mobile customer. She expects personalized customer support on her preferred channel and she expects you to respond now.

The average internet user in the United States spends one hour and 20 minutes online on a personal computer every day.[45] The most connected user group is not your kids, but people who are 50-64 years old (1.6 hours daily), whereas 18-24 year olds spend only an hour online per day using computers. Are young consumers online less than their parents? Of course not. Internet users spend most of their time online on their smartphones and tablets. This especially applies to young consumers, who spend a full four hours a day surfing the web on their phones.[46]

As personalization on a mass scale becomes a generally available technique for companies both small and large, consumers get hammered by hundreds of personalized emails daily and they become numb to them. Spam, or unsolicited email, accounts for as much as 85% of all online

45  Statistica, 2017
46  Statistica, 2017

communication.[47] And although the amount of spam that consumers are exposed to decreases over time with better spam filters, consumers are bombarded by more commercial messages on social media. Companies need to work harder than ever to make their messages relevant, timely and valuable, so they don't get overlooked.

Customer service conversations are both personalized and timely. They are rarely stopped by spam bots or overlooked by the consumer. They have intrinsic value for the customer so they are carefully read. Using customer service conversations as commercial interactions may therefore be more effective for companies than sending another email.

**DIGITAL IS THE FIRST CHOICE FOR GENERATION Y**

Were you born between 1945 and 1960? That means you're probably a big fan of your phone, whether it's a landline or a mobile phone, and you mostly use it when interacting with customer service departments. Not many consumers your age use social media, and most likely you don't often download or use a smartphone app.[48]

Born between 1961 and 1980? Although a phone call is still most likely your favorite way to communicate with customer service, you are almost as likely to use email, SMS or web-based live chat.[49]

Born between 1981 and 1999? Members of your generation are sometimes called Millennials, because you

---

47  "Total Global Email & Spam Volume for July 2018," 2018
48  Arthur D. Little, 2017
49  Arthur D. Little, 2017

were born close to the end of the 21st century. Taking out your smartphone, dialing a customer service hotline and putting your phone to your ear is the least likely option for you. Your behavior and preferred way of communicating is the exact opposite of your older friends and parents. You will most likely use social media or live chat, only followed by email and mobile apps. You belong to the first generation that prefers not to use voice for customer service. Your smartphone lies on the bedside table while you are sleeping, it's the first thing you grab when you wake up, it's with you all day long either beeping and buzzing in the palm of your hand or trying to get your attention in the pocket of your pants. You value a sense of control when communicating with companies. That means having the choice of using a channel you prefer, communicating at a time you choose and not bothering with whether you should start a message with "Dear Sir or Madam" or just "Hi there." You expect brands to accommodate your language tonality and communication style. Because when it comes to your relationship with companies, you want to be in control.[50]

It's important to note that the age-based consumer segmentation presented above is considered by some experts as outdated, since many older people are highly digitally savvy whereas there are certain young consumers who generally do not use digital channels as much.

**The behavior and preferred way of communicating for Millennials is the opposite of their older friends and parents.**

50    Arthur D. Little, 2017

% of centers reporting most popular contact channels by generation

| | INTERNET/WEB CHAT | SOCIAL MEDIA | EMESSAGING | SMARTPHONE APP | TELEPHONE |
|---|---|---|---|---|---|
| **GENERATION Y**<br>(born 1981-1999) | 24%<br>(1st choice) | 24%<br>(1st choice) | 21%<br>(3rd choice) | 19%<br>(4th choice) | 12%<br>(5th choice) |
| **GENERATION X**<br>(born 1961-1980) | 21%<br>(3rd choice) | 12%<br>(4th choice) | 28%<br>(2nd choice) | 11%<br>(5th choice) | 29%<br>(1st choice) |
| **BABY BOOMERS**<br>(born 1945-1960) | 7%<br>(3rd choice) | 2%<br>(5th choice) | 24%<br>(2nd choice) | 3%<br>(4th choice) | 64%<br>(1st choice) |
| **SILENT GENERATION**<br>(born before 1944) | 2%<br>(3rd choice) | 1%<br>(4th choice) | 6%<br>(2nd choice) | 1%<br>(5th choice) | 90%<br>(1st choice) |

Digital channels are the first choice for Generation X, Arthur D.Little, 2017

## RESPOND EVERYWHERE

Having lived in post-socialist Czechoslovakia and later the independent Czech Republic through the late 1980s to the early 21st century before moving to London and later to California, I had the opportunity to see the shift in how people like you and me use their mobile phones. Back in the '90s the first financially accessible mobile phones came into stores, and I saw hundreds of people on the streets with phones attached to their ears talking loudly and waving their hands as if they wanted everyone to know that they were leading the mobile revolution. Typing 160 characters into an SMS was painfully slow when you only had 10 buttons, and my friends at elementary school actually organized a competition to see how fast they could type a sentence on an Alcatel OneTouch handheld. I remember a few of my friends suffered pain in their hands after pushing the phone buttons thousands of times every day. In those days getting through a crowded subway platform during rush hour meant listening to dozens of phone conversations.

Walking on the same platform today, I don't hear any conversations. Not that people no longer use the subway! If you care enough to casually look at the displays of your fellow passengers' smartphones, you can check out who passed the 100th level of Candy Crush Saga, who customized his background image in WhatsApp and who likes to scroll down a Facebook wall using his thumb rather than his first finger. Subway platforms have become quieter as the thousands of words spoken by thousands of voices have moved to glowing smartphone screens.

Whatever device people learned to use to communicate with their friends and colleagues, they have also adapted to communicating with customer service departments when something goes wrong. Contact centers received 14% fewer phone calls in 2017, fueling growth and customer engagement on all other digital channels. By 2020, only 29% of customers will rely on phone channels for support.[51] Fewer phone calls means fewer customer service agents, lower costs, and higher profits, right? Nope.

Phone calls have been replaced by instant messages, Facebook posts, tweets, live chats and video chats. The overall volume of customer service contacts continues to increase because there is a low barrier to picking up a phone and hitting the send button, or opening a mobile app and sending an inquiry. In the past, companies tried to keep their customers rather passive. Today, as you will learn later in these chapters, the benefits of engaging customers are

51   Wiant, 2016

increasing so brands advise their customers to contact them more often, mostly via digital channels. The adoption of new digital channels is mesmerizing: while it took about 75 years for the telephone to reach 50 million users, it only took three and half years for Facebook to do the same. Facebook, the largest social networking site in the world, today reports over two billion active users.[52] But still, Facebook is only one app installed on a smartphone. Where does that leave a contact center agent who used to simply pick up a phone every time a computer told them somebody was on the line? At best, it leaves them uncertain about the future of their job.

> **Digital channels are likely to overtake voice customer service in the next few years.**

As we've seen, research shows that digital channels are likely to overtake voice customer service in the next few years. One channel is being replaced by many. That means responding to an impatient live chat user is completely different from empathetically responding to a complainer sending angry comments to thousands of Facebook followers. And picking up a video chat session while taking control of a desperate customer's internet browser as they're trying to find a decent mobile data package on a website requires not only a patient voice, factual preparation and expert knowledge, but also carefully trimmed hair, a good looking shirt and an attractive office space that will be captured by the webcam streaming live

52  "Number of monthly active Facebook users worldwide as of 1st quarter 2018," 2018

video to the customer in need of a human connection.

So it's logical that Chief Financial Officers ask the Head of Customer Service on a quarterly basis: "How will you save operational costs, which we so desperately need to do, when the number of customer interactions is steadily increasing?" Instead of "optimizing" or "downsizing" the customer service department, CFOs are asked to approve the purchase of new tools, technologies, and trainings as it's repeatedly argued that instead of salary cuts, the company needs to invest more to hire agents to meet the expectations of increasingly demanding customers. Bye bye, profit projections! Au revoir, annual bonuses!

In addition, after that poor Head of Finance got a briefing from his kids at home about Snapchat, WhatsApp and Vine, he came back to work actually looking forward to his next meeting with the Head of Marketing so he could shine for once while discussing how the coolest new trends affect the company's bottom line. So imagine his surprise when the Head of Marketing arrived with more mind-boggling news: "Facebook is no longer just a social media site... Social messaging is now used for voice messages... Customers want to pay their invoices over Facebook and WeChat these days... That super-popular live streaming app called Meerkat you learned about last night doesn't actually exist anymore."

**This whole social and digital thing is too complicated!** And it keeps changing... Yep, now the Head of Finance gets it. What was one phone call picked up by one customer service agent only 15 years ago is today dozens of different communication apps, websites and online services converging their functionality, acquiring their businesses fueled by the funds of bombastic VC investors and coded by headhunted software engineers switching from one employer to another in a radius of just 80 miles in Silicon Valley (or their smaller versions in Berlin, Singapore, London and Stockholm).

> **This whole social and digital thing is too complicated! And it keeps changing...**

## CUSTOMERS DON'T DISTINGUISH BETWEEN B2B AND B2C CHANNELS

Back in the days of telephones, physical branch opening hours and mail delivery times, it was easy to distinguish between customer requests coming from other business customers and those coming from individual consumers. It went something like this:

"Microsoft Inc. calling? All right, patch them to Ralph, our B2B guy." "Jenny, our prepaid customer, is sending a letter? Hand it over to our Mass Market Consumer team, they'll deal with her."

Back then, the lines between Business to Business channels (B2B) and Business to Consumer channels (B2C) were clearly drawn. Today, you've got the Microsoft guy sending a LinkedIn message to his Key Account Manager on Sunday night, then tweeting about it publicly after not getting a response the next day. You've got Jenny patiently studying the pricing differences among a variety of products on a website knowledge base, and going through materials typically meant for business customers only minutes before searching for the right channel to connect with a company via a mobile app. WhatsApp, a social messaging app, is today used not only among peers and friends, but also as a powerful B2B messaging channel for many managers who are too busy to check their overflowing email inboxes. B2B and B2C communication has converged to a large extent on digital channels. Companies are no longer in full control of where their customers will be sent. That means they need to be flexible and smart about how they deal with customers, no matter if they are B2B or B2C.

**ONE-TO-ONE-TO-ONE-TO-MANY**

The differences between "one-to-one," "one-to-many," and "many-to-many" channels are blurring. iMessage, Apple's rich-format SMS equivalent, is not just used for one-to-one conversations, but it's also used as a group chatting channel among many business teams. Facebook, traditionally understood as a "one-to-many" media publishing format used by brands to "stream" messages to maximize "reach" and "brand engagement," is today used as a messaging channel between friends, as a group chatting platform among peers, as a polling channel for collecting consumer insights, as an automated shopping portal powered by chatbot technologies integrated with e-commerce sites, and much more.

# CUSTOMERS ARE GETTING SMARTER WITH THEIR REQUESTS

It's not only that the number and scope of channels has changed, but consumers have changed too, so they're increasingly "smarter" about their requests. McKinsey Research argues that the consumer purchasing decision-making journey has became more sophisticated in recent years due to internet access and the customer's more critical view of branded information.[53]

In this more complicated customer journey, it's no longer just about making the customer aware of your product and familiar with its advantages. Two-thirds of the newly identified touchpoints during the active-evaluation phase involve internet reviews and word-of-mouth recommendations from friends and family. It's important to note that all of these are consumer-driven activities. That means the importance of customer service during the decision-making journey is growing, from 12% during the initial consideration phase to 43% at the time of purchase.[54] Companies need to focus more attention on Customer Value Management and the role of both proactive and reactive customer service in increasing the value of customers. Gone are the days when the sole role of customer service was retaining the customer as long as possible.

53  Court, et. al., 2009
54  Court, et. al., 2017

From the customer's point of view, the increasing access to information about brands and products is coupled with a decrease in trust in those brands. That means customers seek more references and referrals, which in turn makes customer service more important than ever.

**Companies need to focus more attention on Customer Value Management and the role of both proactive and reactive customer service in increasing customer value.**

# IOT MAKES CUSTOMER SERVICE INVISIBLE

Do you know the saying that "the best customer service is no customer service at all?" The Internet of Things (IoT) has been presented by many early adopters and passionate journalists as the next big event in technology. In theory, consumers would no longer have to reach out to contact center agents, as products would seamlessly communicate with manufacturers or service departments without human help. Connected products seamlessly interacting with each other and making our daily lives more comfortable and joyful? It certainly sounds promising!

But still, while I wrote these lines, my editing app crashed a few times. Although I was connected to the internet the whole time, I was required to confirm that I wanted to send an error message to the manufacturer and I had to send an email with a manually written description in order to get the problem sorted out. As I got into my car for the ride home, an icon popped up on dashboard informing me that I needed to change the oil. My internet-connected car informed me that I needed to get to the internet and send a message to my mechanic to book an appointment. Then, while driving to the mechanic, an SMS alert informed me that I had used all my mobile data for the month so I was no longer connected to the internet. In other words, an internet-connected device informed me that my internet connection would no longer work, while my mobile operator, who has my credit card details on file, does nothing but wait until I call the customer service hotline and request additional data.

In this world where autonomous cars are tested in the streets of our cities, where computers beat humans in every logical game, where home thermostats by Nest manage the heating of rooms based on the behavioral patterns of your family, and where planes land softly on the runway thanks to millions of calculations per second delivered by Artificial Intelligence, we still keep calling contact centers with very basic requests!

IoT and internet-connected devices can fundamentally change the future requirements of customer service. The global IoT market is predicted to grow from $157 billion (€135 billion) in 2016 to $457 billion (€395 billion) by 2020.[55] Once the basic use cases outlined above are being solved by the better use of connected products, customers won't stop there. They'll certainly start buying more intelligent connected devices. Picture a refrigerator automatically

55  Columbus, 2017

ordering a home delivery of groceries based on how much milk and yogurt is left in the fridge, or smart door locks opening up when your smartphone is nearby. You'll never again have to remember where you left your keys! Some of these devices are already available on the market and they're becoming increasingly popular.

| IoT and internet-connected devices can fundamentally change the future requirements of customer service.

As self-service has helped reduce the number of incoming calls to contact centers over the past decades, IoT should contribute to a significant reduction of calls in the upcoming decades. We can assume this trend will affect mostly 1st-level customer service dealing with light customer service issues (resetting service, purchasing add-ons, booking appointments, etc.). 2nd and 3rd-level customer issues, which are generally more complex requests that require technical experts, will remain on-demand. Your car booking "a date" with a technician is one thing, but getting its own filters and oil changed is another!

# INCREASING COMPLEXITY REQUIRES EXPERT AGENTS

| 25% of the activities of even exceptional customer service agents will be automated.

As transactional calls and light customer service issues move to digital channels, more complex interactions—many enabling service-to-sales activities—will account for the largest share of volume in traditional call centers. In fact, automation on digital channels will replace some exceptional customer agents. McKinsey predicts that customer service executives will increasingly develop smaller teams comprised of highly skilled agents. If self-service, IoT products and chatbots will take care of all the "change my contact address," "recharge my account" or "where is my package?" requests, will this also affect the demand for expert agents? The simple answer is yes, it will. It's estimated that about 25% of the activities of even exceptional customer service agents will be automated.[56]

Amazon Web Services, the cloud computing provider that's part of Amazon, has already begun to route more technical issues straight to their engineering and product teams, thus bypassing frontline agents. This trend will require highly skilled customer service agents who are capable of providing expert-level support for increasingly complex issues with a high degree of emotional intelligence expected. But many companies aren't ready for this shift. 94% of

56   Berg et. al., 2016

customer service executives mentioned that they needed to hire new agents or train current agents in new skills.[57] Large investments will probably be required to fill the skills gap in recruitment, trainings, and new technologies.

But let's not talk in abstractions. Consider Joe and Jane, average consumers with smartphones buzzing in their pockets. They're driving the decisions in the shiny boardrooms where customer care executives with bespoke suits and Armani shirts are sipping Nespresso. In past centuries, businesses drove consumer demand for new technologies. But today, service businesses with thousands of customer service agents are changing their strategies reactively. Over the past ten years, following the global economic depression of 2008, customer care leaders have spent their days finding any remaining penny to be cut and saved. Offshoring, outsourcing to developing countries, self-service, and Interactive Voice Responders (IVR) are just some of the most common measures. Cut a full-time agent here, lower a salary there, downsize contact center office space here, automate a process there... Savings were necessary for survival and to regain the trust of investors and creditors.

**The better use of customer data and omnichannel customer service will help businesses get more money for the same costs.**

That's about to change. Investing into new technologies is a top priority for almost half of customer care leaders.[58]

57   Berg et. al., 2016
58   Berg et al., 2016

Companies need to invest into integrating channels, and adding new channels, putting funding behind both consumer-facing technologies (such as customer kiosks and mobile apps) and internal systems, such as CRM. While investment is a new thing after a decade of savings, other priorities include many cost-saving initiatives as well, like strengthening self-service or better workforce management and labor cost management. The better use of customer data and omnichannel customer service will help businesses get more money for the same costs, thus improving profitability.

How?

Take Monica. Exhausted, she just put her legs up on her sofa at home on Sunday night after she put five full bags of groceries on the kitchen table and put Willy, her one-year-old son, to bed. Bread, croissants for breakfast, apples and bananas, toiletries, snacks, milk, yogurt and 30 other items, easily adding up to 40 pounds carried by poor Monica one mile from the local Target. And just when she turned on the TV and smiled, thinking that her duties were done for today... the diapers! Damn it! For those who know what it's like to raise small children, you know that no spare diapers means no fun. And just think, this whole situation might have been avoided!

Shopping for groceries online is not a new thing, but it's increasing in popularity lately. The added benefit of shopping on the internet is that retailers save your purchasing preferences, so the otherwise overlooked diapers in the physical store might be easily recommended for an electronic basket when shopping online.

This isn't exactly the high-tech transhuman AI-enabling story you'd expect from the previous chapter, right? Many online grocery stores already offer one-click purchases of frequently bought products. But consider this: any purchasing transaction done in the physical world, when done in the digital world, enables content and product personalization, product recommendations, smart alerting ("home delivery to your location is likely to take an additional hour due to heavy traffic;" "interested in diapers? You have purchased them in the past, but not today;") and the resolution of many frequent customer questions proactively, thus deflecting call demand into the contact center, enabling agents to focus on more complex and empathy-requiring issues. Moreover, the digital experience enables brands to suggest various up-sells and cross-sales opportunities and to inform the customer proactively about recent features and possibilities, therefore making them more educated. You just killed a bunch of birds with one stone. Monica's happy. You're happy. The company has higher profits.

# CHAPTER SUMMARY

Customers have gained more power than ever thanks to recent technological innovations such as smartphones and social media. Many companies have taken advantage of new technologies as well in order to provide better content personalization through big data analytics, more automation through intelligent assistants, chatbots and business process automation. Virtual Reality, Augmented Reality and the Internet of Things will further enable companies to provide a richer customer experience. Traditional call centers will likely be replaced by digitally-focused modern contact centers, as off-shored, poorly educated customer service agents will be replaced by in-house expert advisors.

# CHAPTER 3

# THE
# COMPANIES
# BREAKING
# FROM
# THE PAST

Chapter 2 showed how digital technologies have changed the consumer behavior of today's productive generations and how innovative companies can use recent technologies to provide more efficient customer service and much richer customer experiences. In this chapter, let's take a look at the state most companies are in today regarding their use of technology and automation, and let's think about how every company can move to the next level.

# SERVICE COMPANIES ARE BECOMING COMMODITIES

Companies in competitive markets are becoming increasingly commodified and they now need to compete on the level of customer experience rather than price. Some people don't want to admit it, but service businesses are becoming commodities. Think about it: they're easily replaceable by the next best thing and it can be hard (if not impossible) for customers to find a qualitative difference between one service provider and the next. The electricity that flows through wires to charge your phone, laptop or fridge every night is just electricity. You can't tell whether all the electricity that energized your gadgets today was made at the same power station, and you don't know if the shining light coming from the bulb above your desk originated in the turbines of a wind farm or in a coal mine. Electricity has no brands and no differences in quality.

Customer service is the new electricity. Take telecommunications operators, for example. They all offer pretty much the same thing: fixed-line service, data and calling plans, and prepaid SIM cards. Now take banks: they all offer a standard bank account for an individual, a businessman, a company, a loan here, an overdraft there, and a mortgage for your house.

> **Without a differentiating factor like customer experience, service businesses are left to compete on price and stealing customers.**

Something that may have once been a product differentiator — a superior network — soon becomes the minimum service that customers expect.

Slashing prices and offering one-time incentives to switch telco providers is a short-term approach. One way forward might go something like this: "Do we have the same product as all of our competitors? Then let's outsmart them with marketing!" Sounds good, right? Right! But is it really?Today's highly stimulated customers instinctively and intentionally tune-out traditional advertising, rendering it ineffective. Billboards, TV ads, radio ads, newspaper ads, it's all traditional advertising! Online banners, email newsletters… all traditional advertising as well! According to a 2015 study, 63% of respondents said that they tended to avoid online ads, and 68% said they disliked in-app mobile ads as well.[59]

Customer experience is the main driver of customer service. Gartner predicted that by 2018, more than 50% of organizations would redirect their investments to customer experience innovations.[60] Moreover, the same research also predicted that 89% of companies will soon be competing on the basis of customer experience, though they've offered no recent update revealing to what extent this is now true. But we can clearly see that profitability goes down as companies reach market penetration and offer commoditized products and services. Great customer experience can be that differentiator. What does great customer experience mean? According to a recent survey of 450 senior contact center executives by Deloitte, customer experience is predominantly influenced by providing accurate service and information and by making interactions effortless.[61]

**Great customer service can be a competitive differentiator.**

59   McDermott, 2012
60   Gartner, 2018
61   Deloitte, 2017

# WHY TIME IS OF THE ESSENCE FOR CUSTOMERS

Time is uniquely important in customer service because it fulfills the needs of the customer and the company in both emotional and functional ways. From the business point of view, time is money because more customer queries answered more quickly saves money. In customer service, saving customer time also means saving company time.

**SAVING CUSTOMER TIME**

> **Chatbots help to expand customer service around the clock and can handle thousands of conversations at the same time.**

One of the biggest complaints that customers have about communicating with companies is the time they waste waiting for a response or entering personal information more than once. Saving time makes customers feel better because it appeals to this pain point. Do you remember the last time you called a customer service hotline and the sweet, enthusiastic pre-recorded voice announced that a customer service advisor will be with you shortly—you are the 16th in the line? Damn! How much did you wish that robotic lady on the other end of the line could hear what you were thinking? Well, one of the recent techniques to save customers time waiting for an agent to connect with them is implementing live chat chatbots, so whenever you connect with the company via a web-based live chat or Facebook Messenger, it greets you, collects the specifics of your issue, suggests an appropriate resolution and makes sure you leave satisfied. If the chatbot is incapable of understanding the customer's intent or the issue is just too complex for the poor scripted robot, it seamlessly transfers the customer to available agents. These chatbots are generally available 24/7 and can handle thousands of customers at the same time in various languages and over different channels.

## SAVING COMPANY TIME

When agents work more efficiently they increase productivity without increasing the size of the team. That saves the company money while ensuring more revenue from happier customers. In a recent case study by Makedonski Telekom,[62] a European telecommunications company owned by T-Mobile, and Brand Embassy, a technology company I happened to co-found, the customer service department increased outbound volumes by 1,100%, resolved 3x more cases and improved response times by 200% with no change of employee count. The improved productivity was achieved by a combination of streamlined processes, implementation of intelligent routing and a prioritization algorithm, a simple-to-use ticketing system and improved coaching. Moreover, the company has implemented a chatbot to handle a number of incoming cases automatically.

62 "Case Study: Transforming the CX approach to meet the demand for digital customer interactions," 2018

The recent development of AI-powered technologies has created new opportunities for tools using machine learning and natural language processing (NLP) to provide customer service agents with optimal pre-written responses to increasingly complex customer issues. The technologies, known as Intelligent Advisors, use semantic analysis to understand the subject of the inquiry, while complementary information about the customer is pulled from the internal CRM system and meta data comes with the incoming conversation. Then technologies made to recognize the intent of the conversation are used to select what relevant knowledge base records should be pulled. The computer system then tries to patch various pre-written instructions into sentences, or use whole pre-defined chunks of text so the customer service agent only has to add the finishing touches before it's sent to a customer. The capabilities of the systems depend highly on the quality and scale of the relevant input data and the ability of the machine-learning algorithms. Many implementations fail to be significantly more productive than a well-categorized knowledge base, but it's very likely that the capabilities will continue to improve rapidly in the coming years.

**Intelligent Advisors help human agents to handle more customer inquiries by having their responses drafted by a computer.**

# HOW TO FULFILL CUSTOMERS' EMOTIONAL NEEDS

| **Over 90% of our behavior is generated unconsciously.**

A few years ago, neuroscientist Antonio Damasio made a groundbreaking discovery that changed the perception of the nature of rational thinking and decision making that has dominated scientific thought for centuries. Previous to Damasio's discovery, scientists—himself included—believed that emotions and reason did not mix any more than oil and water. Now, most neuroscientists would agree that well over 90% of our behavior is generated unconsciously.[63]

Damasio studied people with damage in the part of the brain where emotions are generated. He found that they all seemed normal, except that they were not able to feel emotions. These patients had entirely healthy minds— flawless language and the ability to perform calculations or tackle the logic of an abstract problem—but the onset of this neurological disease which ravaged a specific sector of the brain where emotions are generated caused a profound defect in decision making. These patients could describe what they should be doing in logical terms, yet they found it very difficult to make even simple decisions, such as what to eat. Many decisions have both pros and cons—shall I have

63  Damasio, 1994

the chicken or the turkey? With no rational way to decide, these test subjects were unable to arrive at a decision. The research proved that humans in general and therefore customers are driven by emotions when making even the smallest decisions. How does this affect businesses and customer service specifically?

**Customers are driven by emotions when making even the smallest decision.**

Emotionally engaged customers—customers who have positive associations with a brand—are more loyal and more likely to advocate for that brand, compared to customers who are simply satisfied or have no real emotional connection.[64] A recent study by the Harvard Business Review shows that emotionally connected customers are 25-100% more valuable than just "highly satisfied customers."[65] Moreover, 74% of customers with positive emotions will advocate, while 63% will be retained, however only 8% of customers with negative emotions will advocate for your company and only 13% will be retained.[66] It pays, literally, to have emotionally connected customers because those customers will spend more, promote the brand to other customers and stick around longer.

Still, it's surprisingly easy to forget about how customers feel in the result-driven working environment where KPIs, SLAs, OKRs and other performance metrics determine who gets paid more, who gets promoted and who needs to leave the company. Measuring whether a customer received

64  Delbos, 2018
65  Magids, et. al., 2015
66  Delbos, 2018

a response after 20 minutes is easier than measuring how they felt after they engaged with a customer service representative.

Analyzing and working with the emotions of customers and customer service agents in a way that creates the best customer experiences will be increasingly important as AI and super-intelligent computer programs take over more and more of the tasks traditionally performed by humans. Just like IVRs and answering machines were able to take human agents out of the equation a few decades ago, chatbots and self-service apps have been doing the same more recently. But what the automated solutions are missing is emotional intelligence, which helps human customer service agents respond with the appropriate emotional tonality and adjust the way an issue is handled. Let's dive into the topic of how to work with customer emotions and what business impact this may bring.

> **Analyzing and working with the emotions of customers and customer service agents will be increasingly important.**

Stressed customers who reach out to customer service are generally in an emotional state that is best handled by human agents rather than bots. Emotional customers appreciate accessibility and the fact that a company is available to help in the channel, time and occasion of the customer's choosing. Moreover, a high level of transparency helps to cool down the customer's stress by acknowledging the situation and showing the customer that you appreciate their time and are making an effort to resolve the problem. Finally, as you have learned earlier in this book, customers in an emotional state expect a result-driven approach that leads to a fast resolution without unnecessary promises. These tactics are hard to replicate by robotic conversation and therefore conversations like these should be handled primarily by human agents. Furthermore, human advisors can, unlike chatbots or IVRs, express genuine interest in the customer's inquiry and can be flexible in the flow of the conversation by being guided by empathy rather than a strict conversation script.

## Highly emotional customers are better handled by human agents.

As you know very well, retaining a loyal customer is easier than acquiring a new one. However, companies stress and frustrate customers in many ways. Nearly half of customers say they will stop doing business with a brand that frustrates them.[67] Meanwhile only 32% of those customers will contact the company to complain before taking their business elsewhere. Making customers feel engaged and soothing their frustrations are vital prerequisites for customer loyalty. Customers are 5x more loyal when they feel valued.[68] Over many years working with highly emotional customers across more than 30 countries, I have identified five key desired emotional states that drive loyalty in customer service.

67  Delbos, 2018
68  Delbos, 2018

## 1. SURPRISE

Do you know people who don't like surprises? I'm one of them. I hate surprises. Mostly because I feel uncomfortable being in a situation that's out of my control. However, when it comes to customer service situations I need to resolve, I'm immediately in an uncomfortable situation because it's out of my control! So surprising me positively with a quick response, efficiency, personalization and going the extra mile to make me happy is a necessity. There's still plenty of room for improvement for most companies where digital customer service is concerned, so anything that's extraordinary will surprise customers. Technology helps—agents can retrieve personal customer information from CRM to be used in friendly conversation; can pull relevant additional information by using Intelligent Advisors or a well-categorized knowledge base; or they can make the entire experience richer for the customer by using a variety of channels at the same time when appropriate.

## 2. FAMILIARITY

When something doesn't work or the customer is under time pressure, they seek a familiar environment and experience in order to feel back in control. That's why emotional customers reaching out to a customer service agent do expect to be in touch with a human rather than a bot. Also, offering a scripted resolution or links to self-service articles to customers at such times is typically counterproductive, as it might deepen the customer's frustration even though the actual process of solving the issue may appear efficient. Familiarity might also be achieved by using technologies and interfaces that the customers already have experience with. Note that AI chatbots and automated advisors might still be efficiently utilized at the backend where human agents prepare optimal responses and seek appropriate inputs for conversation.

## 3. RELIEF

No matter how serious the emotional state of a customer is when initiating a conversation with customer service, she wants to feel better when ending the conversation. Even when a situation cannot be resolved right away, the customer wants to feel relieved that things are going to improve and they want to feel informed about the process of getting back on track. How to make it happen? It helps to know if your customer service agents are naturally empathetic. It's also a training issue. Customer service agents should be given some freedom to respond to emotional and conversational cues. From a technological perspective, both conversational bots or AI-powered computational assistants may effectively prepare responses informing the customer about any progress and steps to be taken in order to resolve an issue. In many ways, appointing a human agent or humanized bot that acknowledges responsibility for getting the issue solved may also help the customer feel relieved.

## 4. GRATITUDE

By receiving a positive surprise, a high degree of familiarity and the feeling of relief, the customer is on a good path to staying with the company. By adding the element of gratitude, the customer will remain loyal and possibly share positive brand experiences with peers. The feeling of being grateful is strong when shared mutually between people. When a human agent feels grateful for the time they've spent with the customer, there is a good chance the customer will feel grateful towards the human agent for the genuine efforts the agent put into making her happy again. It's an altogether different situation when the dehumanized approach of current chatbot technologies or automated voice responders falls short in comparison to emphatic humans. Unless the computer programs can apply the same degree of emotional intelligence in order to create a sense of gratitude, it's better to stay away from even trying.

## 5. BELONGING

"Hey Jack, are u coming back again? Looking good today! What's new?" The feeling of entering a friendly space and being welcomed by the staff of a local brick and mortar shop down the street is hard or maybe impossible to replicate in the digital world or over the phone. However, friendly communities do exist in virtual worlds. One customer service-related example are the community forums that serve as peer-to-peer discussion platforms moderated or administered by brands. Another example are branded social media pages. In these cases, customers may feel like they're part of a larger community of consumers. If the brand acknowledges that fact it may help to improve the emotional state of the customer. Moreover, some social media groups are actually handled by expert consumers or so-called "brand advocates" or "super users." Smart community-focused technologies may suggest connecting the customer to the most appropriate subject-matter experts or directing the customer to the already existing community of users with similar past requirements.

Companies need to focus more on the emotional intelligence of customers and human customer service agents in order to strengthen customer loyalty and avoid customer churn. AI-powered technologies will be increasingly used to assist humans to respond to customer emotions appropriately. Although a variety of technologies focused on voice channels is available on the market, much broader capabilities are now being developed for digital, written channels. With the growing trend of consumers switching to digital channels, companies need to incorporate consumer expectations towards digital. Let's take a look at where they are today.

# COMPANIES ARE FALLING BEHIND WITH DIGITAL

Here's the chicken and egg problem. Although highly intelligent digital technologies that improve both customer satisfaction and company bottom-lines are widely accessible on the market, they are not sufficiently used. Companies fail to implement them and customers do not use them enough either. Should companies wait for customers to motivate them strongly to innovate, or should customers wait on companies to give them more convenient means of shopping and being taken care of?

It's the opinion of the author that companies need to take the leap of faith and invest into providing better digital capabilities for their customers. Why? Because they know they should. Even the smallest startup company can easily collect direct customer feedback in real-time and analyze the optimal communication channels, desired customer use cases and the product offerings their consumers are asking for. Implementing them is a business responsibility. In many cases however, as you will learn in the upcoming pages, companies are failing to bring digital to life.

While customers already use digital channels, as indicated in the previous chapter, companies are falling behind and still excessively rely on traditional channels. To take a look at mobile operators for example, generally well-established enterprises offer a variety of digital products to mass markets, but only 13% of all digital interactions processed by mobile operators are service-based, and customers do not generally use digital. Although consumers frequently use digital channels for day-to-day activities, with 69% reading online news and 59% using online banking, only 10-15% connect with their mobile operator by using digital channels in order to resolve their issues. Out of those, the largest group (30%) renew and purchase new services, and roughly one in four consumers pays their monthly bills online. Fewer than one in eight consumers uses digital channels to resolve customer service inquiries, as mentioned earlier.[69]

Is it because both customers and companies don't actually want to use these channels? I don't think so. Look at how we use digital gadgets and software in almost every part of our daily lives. Is it because the technologies would be too hard for the companies to implement or too costly? That might be partially true, because bringing change to large enterprises is generally quite time consuming, as every corporate manager will confirm. However, blaming slow corporate processes for a lack of business innovation would be too shortsighted. Technology vendors are also partially to blame, as some pretty smart niche technologies lack seamless integration into the wider technology stack, and large-scale technologies are sometimes clunky and not easy to implement.

**DIGITAL CLIENTS BEHAVIORS**

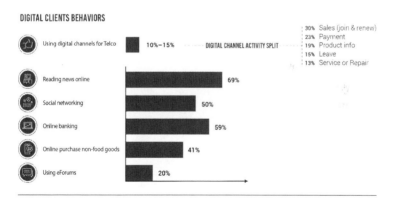

| | | |
|---|---|---|
| Using digital channels for Telco | 10%–15% | DIGITAL CHANNEL ACTIVITY SPLIT |

- 30% Sales (join & renew)
- 23% Payment
- 19% Product info
- 15% Leave
- 13% Service or Repair

| | |
|---|---|
| Reading news online | 69% |
| Social networking | 50% |
| Online banking | 59% |
| Online purchase non-food goods | 41% |
| Using eForums | 20% |

McKinsey, 2016

69  McKinsey,2016

## THE PROBLEM WITH SELF-SERVICE

For many years, many people believed self-service was the answer to the ever-growing expense of customer service and the increasing impatience of customers. It apparently makes sense—as customers get smarter with their requests, they are not shy in seeking resolutions to their requests by themselves online. If companies published relevant, easy to search and digest information on their websites, why wouldn't a consumer scared of being stuck on a consumer hotline take care of herself? Although it does make sense and many consumers use online self-service forums, publicly accessible web-based knowledge bases or self-service mobile apps, many find the self-service less helpful than they would wish. Recent research by Youbiquity shows that 72% of banking customers using self-service rated the process as "not easy."

In addition, 28% of complaining customers said that the online self-service process failed, and another 37% said they needed to contact the organization in other ways. Overall, 69% of customers contacted the company more than twice when trying to resolve a complaint.[70]

Clearly, self-service is actually making many customer service-related issues costly and inefficient while also making customers dissatisfied. Businesses should use self-service as an addition to human-based customer service and conversation-based bots that can use the same self-service resources. But they should be put into a more easily digestible form for the regular impatient customer and

70   Youbiquity, 2016

companies should always have a human advisor one click away to help a consumer whose emotions get too high.

> **Businesses should use self-service as an addition to human-based customer service and conversation--based bots.**

| DONE IN THE LAST 18 MONTHS | | OF THOSE, % TRIED TO RESOLVE PROBLEM WITH DIGITAL SELF SERVICE | % SAYING ONLINE PROCESS FAILED | OR NEEDED TO CONTACT ORG. IN OTHER WAYS | HOW MANY TIMES CONTACTED THE ORGANIZATION | | RATING NOT EASY |
|---|---|---|---|---|---|---|---|
| | | | | | 2 to 4 | 5 or more | |
| Made an appointment to see finalcial advisor | 10% | 28% | 9% | 38% | 29% | 6% | **25%** |
| Made your investments online | 5% | 81% | 5% | 23% | 28% | 7% | **48%** |
| Made policy change to car or home insurance | 24% | 41% | 12% | 36% | 31% | 5% | **29%** |
| Made a complaint | 7% | 52% | 28% | 37% | 38% | 31% | **72%** |

Digital self-service interactions often fail consumers, Youbiquity, 2016

# THE EFFECTS OF NEW TECHNOLOGY ON CUSTOMER SERVICE

When it comes to the future of customer service there are basically two competing opinions. Some experts say: "The days are numbered for human customer service agents! Robots will take all our jobs." Others say: "Computers will never match the ever-growing expectations of customers!

Humans will prevail." Let's take a look at both of these opinions and try to chart the way forward for companies, customers and service agents.

## FIRST-LEVEL CUSTOMER SERVICE WILL BE AUTOMATED

As the previous chapters have made clear, it's no longer a question whether customer service will be automated, it's only a question of how much and when.

A recent Tata Consultancy Services survey shows that almost a third of major companies are now using AI in customer service.[71] In the customer service industry, Merchant Bank, a leading credit card issuer in China, handles 1.5-2 million customer inquiries on a daily basis by using an automated chatbot, eliminating the need for hiring hundreds of customer service agents.[72] And more banks across the world are launching their versions of intelligent bots or advisors: Erica was brought to life by Bank of America, providing account balance information, sending notifications and handling basic customer service requests. Ally Bank, another American consumer bank, was one of the first to offer virtual assistant support with its Ally Assist bot available in their mobile banking application. And you can go to the website of your own bank and most likely you'll find their version of a virtual assistant.

Based on research, case studies of technology disrupters, and first-hand experience in the customer

---

71  "Artificial Intelligence to Have Dramatic Impact on Business by 2020, According to Tata Consultancy Services Global Trend Study," 2017
72  Moloney, 2017

service technology market, I assume that all customer service activities will be automated at some point, excluding only two categories of requests: complex requests that require creativity or interpersonal skills, and those requiring empathy and a high degree of emotional intelligence. This is especially true for first-level customer service, or light customer service issues in which agents do not deal with a high level of technical expertise.

> **Customer service will be fully automated with the exception of complex and empathy-requiring issues.**

## PROTECTED REVENUES THROUGH OMNICHANNEL EXPERIENCE

The omnichannel mantra has been a part of the discussions of virtually every customer service expert around the world for many years. Use the keyword "omnichannel" in response to any random customer service-related question and chances are, you are going to impress your colleagues. A little harder follow-up question might be, what do you actually mean by omnichannel, as the word can have so many different meanings for day-to-day business. Most experts would generally agree that omnichannel customer experience means that customers get the same level, scope and quality of experience regardless of the communication channel they have used. For those readers bored by theoretical definitions I offer you a simple explanation: "Thank you for your question, this channel is not used for customer service, contact us at 800-234-123" means bad customer service. "Thank your for your questions sent to our email, our assistant will call your telephone shortly" is slightly better, and is often called multichannel customer service. And "Thank your for your question, let me help you here and now..." is omnichannel customer service. You can easily judge which makes you feel most appreciated.

> **Poor customer service is a leading reason for customer churn.**

Now, let's talk about the effects of omnichannel for business. The link between poor customer service and churn is clear. How clear? Well, Oracle's Customer Experience Impact Report[73] reveals that the two central reasons customers leave a company are rude, incompetent staff, and slow service. In addition, according to Forum Cooperation, poor service is the reason for 70% of customer churn.[74]

In addition, McKinsey shows that across industries, successful projects for optimizing customer experience typically achieve revenue growth of 5% to 10% and cost reductions of 15% to 25% within just two or three years. Moreover, companies offering an exceptional customer experience can exceed the gross margins of their competitors by more than 26% while they make their employees happier and simplify their end-to-end operations.[75]

Research from Gartner suggests that the right omnichannel approach can reduce customer frustration and improve loyalty.

73   Customer Experience Impact Report, 2011
74   Plaksij, 2018
75   McKinsey, 2017

According to a study by Forrester,[76] digital touchpoints affect approximately 49% of total U.S. retail sales. Additionally, a Nielsen consumer survey found that stores with digital signs near checkout lines, for example, have witnessed increases in sales of up to 33%.[77]

Although implementing omnichannel customer experience can be a painful process for a business of any size (and generally more painful as the business grows), the positives are clear. With the increasing use of AI and machine learning technologies the financial benefits of omnichannel are growing steadily.

**Companies offering exceptional CX exceed competition by 26% in margins.**

# NEW REVENUES THROUGH SERVICE TO SALES

Now, let's talk money. And I mean real business. As customers move from traditional to digital channels, companies risk losing revenues that have been traditionally generated on upsells and cross sales via voice calls. "And now, Frank, since we just fixed your problem, why don't you take a look at our newest iPhone?" For

76   NRF, 2018
77   Nielson, 2018

a telecommunications company in Europe with 10 million phone calls in the call center each year, this risk is as high as $148 million (€128 million), according to recent research by McKinsey.[78] For many companies, that's the difference between staying profitable or going under. Moreover, as customers increasingly use digital channels more frequently than phones, it is estimated that an additional $83 million (€72 million) can be generated through the efficient use of digital channels for so-called Service to Sales opportunities.[79]

What is Service to Sales? Ask any financial director in any big company what customer service means to her, and she'll respond "Cost!" Ask startup founders or small company owners what customer service means to them and many will respond "An opportunity! To build loyalty, to build trust, to sell more." Not that some smart people in enterprises wouldn't get it, but contact center departments in enterprises are to be found in Cost of Sales lines on balance sheets. That means heads of finance, as explained earlier, are doing everything they can to cut the customer service cost as much as they can, so they can invest more into sales and marketing. Moreover, customer service agents are not hired with the expectation of building value for the company, but rather of causing the smallest harm by staying low, not costing too much and picking up and hanging up phones quickly so they can deal with as many customers as possible. That's a traditional view of customer service.

Service to Sales, on the contrary, is a concept where customer service is considered as a revenue-generating

78   McKinsey, 2017
79   McKinsey, 2017

business unit. Selling through caring. The idea is simple: Since customers now spend less and less time with brands, the opportunity to build long-lasting relationships is very limited. Customers who have an issue, however, don't hesitate to contact the brand and have a discussion. This is an amazing opportunity for the company to not only turn a dissatisfied customer into a loyal supporter, but also to recommend relevant products and sell more.

Service to Sales can be more efficient in generating sales than marketing. Unlike an online banner that has been displayed to a customer based on her previous product interest during her last website visit (in the best-case scenario), a customer service agent has the opportunity to actually speak with the customer. They can ask follow-up questions, identify real interests and desires and drive the conversation to the most relevant product or service offered on the most relevant terms for the customer. That's CRM on steroids.

| **Service to Sales can be more efficient in generating sales than marketing.**

| CONTACTS PER YEAR | | | SALES CONVERSION RATE | REVENUE GENERATION |
|---|---|---|---|---|
| Traditional CC & IVR | ▓▓▓▓▓ ···· 2X-4X MORE ·····( | | 3%–5% | 128M EUR |
| | **At Risk** - through migration to eCare | | | |
| Digital channel contacts | ▓▓▓▓▓▓▓▓▓▓ | | 0.5%–1.5% | 74M EUR |
| | **White Spot** - not currently addressed | | | |

McKinsey, 2017 – Telecommunications companies can generate an additional €74 million ($86.4 million) by leveraging the potential of Service to Sales through digital channels. McKinsey, 2017

Customer service agents can leverage their access to detailed customer service profiles and previously purchased products, and get automatically advised what "Next best product to buy," or they can determine on their own what are the best product matches for the customer. All this can be done easily within a few seconds while the customer is being assigned within a live chat conversation, a video call or a messaging session.

Moreover, with the rapidly growing capabilities of AI and Natural Language Processing, many of these conversations can be proactively initiated by chatbots while a customer is browsing the website, and relevant recommendations and questions can initiate a valuable discussion. Service to Sales is an opportunity for companies to generate revenue through customer service. It's an opportunity currently overlooked by many companies. Next time you deal with customer service, ask yourself: "Has the company used this unique opportunity for building a relationship with me? Have they offered me something I can't wait to have?"

# CHAPTER SUMMARY

Service businesses are gradually becoming commodities, with customer experience as the competitive differentiator. Timely and empathetic customer service can provide long-lasting positive experiences that lead to higher revenues and customer retention. Businesses should focus on the effective use of currently available technologies to build omnichannel customer service that helps to automate light customer service inquiries and leverage Service to Sales opportunities.

CHAPTER 4

# WILL MACHINES TAKE YOUR JOB?

In the last chapters we considered how technology can improve customer service, leading to more savings and profits. So it would seem like the more technology and automation brands can use, the better. But this leads to the question: if computers can do a better job than human customer service agents, will all those agents soon lose their jobs? It's quite a bit more complex than that, however. This chapter will tease out the complexities of customer service automation and draw some clear distinctions between the abilities of human agents and what computers can do better.

Imagine it's just another weekday. Monday, 8 am. You come to work, sit at your desk and sip freshly brewed coffee while turning on your PC. A few minutes later, after opening a spreadsheet to work on an unfinished report for your boss, you check for new messages on a mail app and open Slack to ask your colleagues what they're doing for lunch.

Then you pick up a phone and talk to a few business partners and customers. As emails keep pouring in, your respond to a few. A colleague from Finance stops by to discuss the monthly report that's due this Friday. At 11 am, Martha, your new intern from Bilbao, Spain, comes to ask for more work because she's already prepared a presentation for your boss, God bless her! When you finally have a spare minute while you sip your second morning coffee, you open up this book, look at this page and feel indignant when the author has the gall to say: Everything you have done so far this morning could be done by a computer. Your apparently important job can be replaced by that piece of plastic and metal sitting at your desk. Sorry!

**How dare he, or, er, how dare I?** But what have you done today that's so unique or complex that artificial intelligence, a robot or the newest computer couldn't do without you? Sending emails? That's so '90s. Gmail is now capable of drafting surprisingly accurate responses by automatically analyzing the content of incoming messages. Ok, what about talking on the phone? Interactive Voice Responders that are capable of guiding callers to an appropriate action have been used by practically every large company for over two decades. Their capabilities have recently been enriched by voice recognition systems, and AI-powered intelligent responders. Besides, your computer doesn't need two coffees every morning, doesn't require lunch breaks, and will never ask your boss for a sick day.

Just another weekday. Except it's your last day at work.

How can you stop this process and get your job back under control? Your best chance to keep doing the work you like is to keep coaching and managing your interns, keep building relationships with your customers and keep seeking new challenges that stretch your creative and cognitive skills. **I invent and improvise, therefore I am.**

> **A computer doesn't need two coffees every morning, doesn't require lunch breaks, and will never ask your boss for a sick day.**

Still, your job might be even more secure than many of your colleagues and peers. There are over 14 million contact center agents picking up phones and responding to incoming customer chats from Buenos Aires to Dallas, from Madrid to Belgrade, Kuala Lumpur to New Delhi and even the city where you are right now. In the United States alone, there are over 2.5 million agents making about $17 (€14.70) an hour. American contact centers have hired over 800,000 workers over the past five years, and more jobs are expected to be created because the Trump administration is pushing American companies to bring jobs back to the home market. Offshoring and outsourcing companies had billed close to $80 billion (€69 billion) by 2016, roughly 12% of what was generated in the United States.[80]

> **There are over 14 million contact center agents globally, and their industry will fundamentally change due to automation.**

80  "Business Process Outsourcing Industry Worldwide—Statistics & Facts"

**Could the entire $80 billion (€69 billion) customer service industry, which employs over 14 million people, simply disappear due to automation and computerization?**

The short answer is no. The entire customer service industry will not disappear. However, it is more than likely that the industry will be fundamentally changed due to automation, Artificial Intelligence and overall technological advancement in the upcoming decades. Let's first dive into the relevant historical parallels that can help us understand the possible impact of this change before discussing what you, or anyone else working in the customer service industry, can do to hang onto your job.

# A HISTORY OF TECHNOLOGICAL ADVANCEMENT

Throughout history, industries have changed, putting millions of workers out of their jobs. Think of how many horse drivers lost their jobs when the car was invented. Or all the bank tellers that were made redundant when ATMs gained popularity. And there are many more examples of this phenomenon, from heavy industry to education and services.

## UNSKILLED WORKERS MAKE WAY FOR WHITE COLLARS

The first assembly line was documented in 1804, but it took nearly another hundred years before the process was adopted on a large scale. This enabled the Ford Motor Company to produce its Model T automobile at such a low price that it became known as "the people's vehicle."[81]

The same trend of replacing unskilled manual workers with industrial automation can be traced to the switch to electricity from steam and water power. With companies increasingly adopting continuous-process manufacturing and batch-production methods, the demand for unskilled hands decreased and employers began searching for skilled and educated white-collar non-production workers.[82]

## COMPUTERIZATION MADE TELEPHONE OPERATORS REDUNDANT

At the beginning of the 20th century, office computers increased the demand for clerks.[83] As computers shrank and were moved from large computer rooms to smaller and more affordable spaces, the cost per computation declined by 37% annually between 1945 and 1980.[84] This proved to be a negative trend for telephone operators, many of whom were made redundant. In the 1960s General Motors introduced the first industrial robot and in the 1970s

81   Mokyr, 1990
82   Goldin and Katz, 1998
83   Chandler, 1977; Goldin and Katz, 1998
84   Nordhaus, 2007

self-service technologies gained popularity, with airline reservation systems leading the way.[85]

## HI EXCEL, BYE TYPISTS

Between 1980 and 2000, computing costs decreased even more rapidly, by an average of 64% annually,[86] which led to a surge of computational power and new automation capabilities available to businesses. The first personal computers were introduced in the early 1980s, as the first word processing and spreadsheet programs began to eliminate jobs for typists and those jobs requiring repetitive calculations.[87]

**❙ Computers help you earn more and get more educated.**

I know what you're thinking: Bad computers, stealing human jobs! But could it be that computers help make our jobs more meaningful and better paid? According to Krueger,[88] workers using a computer earn roughly 10 to 15 percent more than those who don't, and using a computer makes it more likely that you'll seek further education. Think about it: computers help you earn more and motivate your kids to go to school. Not bad!

85  Gordon, 2012
86  Nordhaus, 2007
87  Gordon, 2012
88  Krueger, 1993

## ROBOTS ARE TAKING OVER

Technological progress has two competing effects on employment.[89] First, there's a destructive effect as technology replaces human labor, requiring workers to find new jobs in other roles or industries. Second, there's the capitalization effect, as more companies enter industries where productivity is relatively high, leading to new jobs and the expansion of the industry.

| Technology requires workers to adapt to new job conditions and helps to create new jobs.

## BYE BYE, ROUTINE JOBS

As opposed to the dominant trends of the 19th and 20th centuries, when unskilled blue collar workers had to re-educate and find jobs requiring higher skills that weren't susceptible to automatization, in the early 21st century we're going through the opposite trend. Now, highly skilled workers have moved down the occupational ladder, taking on jobs traditionally performed by unskilled workers.[90]

89   Aghion and Howitt, 1994
90   Benedikt and Osborne, 2013

> **Skilled workers have begun to take the jobs of unskilled workers. Computerization is now spreading to non-routine jobs.**

According to Brynjolfsson and McAfee,[91] the pace of technological innovation is increasing all the time. More sophisticated softwares and internet services are disrupting the labor market and making workers redundant. As opposed to the industrial revolution and the early days of the computer in the late 20th century, computerization is now spreading to domains commonly defined as non-routine.[92] The essay "Lousy and Lovely Jobs"[93] captures the current trend of labor market polarization, with growing employment in high-income creative and cognitive jobs, and low-income manual occupations, accompanied by a hollowing out of routine middle-income jobs.

This trend is illustrated by the recent advancements of robotic technology: As the costs of robots decline and technological capabilities expand, we can expect robots to gradually substitute for laborers in a wide range of low-wage service occupations, where most American job growth has occurred over the past decades.[94] This means that many low--wage manual jobs that have previously been protected from computerization could disappear over time. But could that be a good thing?

91   Brynjolfsson and McAfee, 2011
92   Benedikt and Osborne, 2013
93   Goos and Manning, 2007
94   Autor and Dorn, 2013

## SOFTWARE IS EATING THE WORLD

If you've committed a crime and are about to go to court, make a wish that your case will come up after lunch. As the Nobel-winning behavioral psychologist Daniel Kahneman has revealed, Israeli judges are substantially more generous in their rulings following their lunch break. Because of behavioral biases like this one, the computerization of cognitive tasks is getting more popular. A software algorithm can be designed to ruthlessly satisfy the small range of tasks it is given. Humans, in contrast, must fulfill a range of tasks unrelated to their occupation, such as eating and sleeping, as mentioned earlier, which necessitate occasional sacrifices in occupational performance.[95]

As Marc Andreessen, a startup founder turned successful investor, noted in 2011, software is eating the world. Six decades into the computer revolution, four decades since the invention of the microprocessor, and two decades into the rise of the modern internet, all of the technology that's required to transform industries through software is finally working and can be widely delivered on a global scale. As Andreessen noted, the cost of a customer running a basic internet application was approximately $150,000 (€130,000) a month back in 2000, while running that same application nowadays in Amazon's cloud costs about $1,500 (€1,300) a month.[96] Today, the most valued taxi company, Uber, is a software company. The largest retailer, Amazon, is a software company. The same applies to hospitality with

95  Kahneman et. al., 1982
96  Andreessen, 2011

142

Airbnb, and media with Facebook. Maybe software really is eating the world. But is technological progress inevitable?

## THE QUEEN SAID NO

A cynical person might say that software engineers and risk-averse startup founders backed by millions of dollars from greedy venture capitalists are in control of our job security. The reality is not that simple. As Schumpeter pointed out 50 years ago,[97] powerful social and economic interests challenge the technological status quo and open the doors to technological innovation. In the UK back in 1589, William Lee, the inventor of the stocking frame knitting machine, was invited to meet with Queen Elizabeth I to discuss his vision of relieving workers of the arduous task of hand-knitting. Seeking patent protection for his invention, he moved to London and rented a building for his innovative machine. To his great disappointment, the Queen was concerned with the impact of his invention and refused to grant the patent, claiming that she had to "consider what the invention could do to my poor subjects. It would assuredly bring them to ruin by depriving them of employment, thus making them beggars."[98] In fact, opposition to Lee's invention was so intense that he had to leave Britain. What this story illustrates is that a technological innovation does not automatically change the labor market. The technology needs social and political support, otherwise even the best innovation will meet a quick end.

97   Schumpeter, 1962
98   Acemoglu and Robinson, 2012

But some carefully regulated industries have changed significantly over the past few years, due to our increasing reliance on technology. One good example is the banking industry, where fraud detection, which was traditionally handled by fraud managers, analysts and bank advisors, has been almost entirely taken over by algorithms. Although, or perhaps because fraud detection is a complex activity, requiring impartial decision-making and the ability to detect trends on a large scale, computers have proven to be more efficient than human experts.[99]

Another example is the energy industry: the cities of Doha, São Paulo and Beijing use sensors on pipes, pumps and other water infrastructure to monitor conditions and manage water loss, reducing leaks by 40 to 50%. In the near future, inexpensive sensors on light poles, sidewalks, and other public property will be installed to capture sounds and images, likely reducing the number of workers in law enforcement.[100]

Last but not least, take the popular transportation and taxi business: an industry heavily under the influence of trade unions is shaking in its foundations because of sharing economy companies such as Uber and Lyft. Although professional taxi drivers are lobbying hard against Uber and other ride-sharing apps to stop their massive expansion plans (and to some extent they have succeeded, with the UK and Germany just two of the markets where Uber services have been banned or significantly reduced recently), companies in the sharing economy have already permanently altered

99  Phua, et al., 2010
100 McKinsey Global Institute, 2013

the industry. Think of all the mothers on maternity leave, the seniors on pensions who need to make more money to live comfortably, and the unemployed graduates searching for jobs who can now just download an app, take a seat in their own automobile and make a decent living by providing a service that was for many years considered a complex job for skilled, trained and certified professionals.

And has the consumer won as well? Ask a mom who needs to take her kid to a tennis tournament on time when the bus just left the stop, or a student leaving a club on Saturday after public transport has stopped running. Costs are down, quality and safety are similar to a traditional taxi, and accessibility is much higher than ever before. Thank technology and the public popularity of these services.

But just because an activity can be automated doesn't mean that it will be—broader economic factors are at play. Jobs that are generally performed by unskilled workers with lower-than-average salaries are less susceptible to automation due to simple economics—businesses would rather focus their attention on automating highly paid jobs, as mentioned earlier, or cutting thousands of jobs at a company at once, thus fundamentally reducing costs. So don't be surprised if the doors at your local Four Seasons hotel are still opened by a smiling doorman, while the accounting department at your company finds itself looking for a new job.

**30% OF WORK WILL BE AUTOMATED FOR 60% OF JOBS**

McKinsey has shown that current technologies could automate 45% of the activities people are paid to perform, and that about 60% of all occupations could see 30% or more of their constituent activities automated.[101] While automation will eliminate very few occupations entirely in the next decade, it will affect portions of almost every job to some degree.

But it might surprise you to hear that automation actually increases employment. For example, the large-scale deployment of bar-code scanners and associated point--of-sale (POS) systems in the United States in the 1980s reduced labor costs per store by an estimated 4.5%, and the cost of the groceries by 1.4%. It also enabled a number of innovations, as well as increased promotions. But cashiers were still needed; in fact, their employment grew at an average rate of more than 2% between 1980 and 2013.[102]

**Automation will affect portions of almost every job to some degree.**

101 McKinsey, 2016
102 Basker, 2015

# IT'S GOOD TO BE A BOSS

McKinsey has analyzed thousands of work activities across hundreds of jobs and has examined the technical feasibility of automation for each. Several factors were identified as drivers of automation affecting the labor market: Technical feasibility, cost to automate, relative scarcity, skills, and costs of workers who might otherwise do the activity, as well as benefits (e.g., superior performance) of automation beyond labor-cost substitution, and regulatory and social--acceptance considerations. As their extensive research shows, the jobs most susceptible to automation are those that are to a large extent performed in a predictable physical environment (think factory warehouse); those that contain a high degree of data processing (think data analyst); and those that require data collection (think a bank advisor giving you forms to apply for a mortgage). Jobs less susceptible to automation are performed in unpredictable physical environments (think a classroom full of grammar school pupils); jobs that include a high degree of stakeholder interaction (think a customer service agent); jobs that require the application of expertise in decision-making, planning and creative tasks (think the art director in an advertising agency); and managerial jobs (think your boss).

## TOP SPOTS FOR AUTOMATION

Generally, it's good not to be in food service or accommodation these days—73% of the activities workers perform in these industries have the potential for automation, based on technical considerations. Of all the sectors examined, the technical feasibility of automation is lowest in education, at least for now, which makes teachers and professors uniquely positioned to be a shining example of how people can protect their jobs. Education could, after all, become a desired and increasingly remunerated industry. Education is also one of the important reasons why human labor has prevailed. Educated workers have a higher ability to acquire new skills[103] that are not yet easily handled by computers. Yet as computerization enters more cognitive domains due to a rapid increase in Artificial Intelligence and Machine Learning capabilities, it will become increasingly more challenging even for educated workers to remain safe from automation.[104]

Interestingly, highly paid professionals won't be spared the dangers of automation. People whose annual incomes exceed $200,000 (€173,000) spend some 31% of their time doing repetitive administrative tasks that could already be mostly automated.[105] Will this all lead to much lower employment, with billions of people losing their jobs? Not necessarily. The benefits of automation may come not from reducing labor costs and laying off workers but from raising productivity through fewer errors, higher output, and improved quality, safety, and speed, as we saw above.

103 Goldin and Katz, 2009
104 Brynjolfsson and McAfee, 2011
105 McKinsey Quarterly, 2016

# COGNITIVE AND SOCIAL SKILLS WILL PROTECT CUSTOMER SERVICE AGENT JOBS, FOR NOW

On one hand, any customer service agent could be replaced by automation. Customer service jobs require cognitive and social skills, similar to retail salespeople, who have a 47% technical potential to be automated, as research shows.[106] Customer service professionals who train or manage other team members are less likely to see their job fundamentally transformed in the near future. The hardest activities to automate with currently available technologies are those that involve managing and developing people (9% automation potential) or those that apply expertise to decision-making, planning, or creative work (18%).[107]

On the other hand, there is a straightforward yet significant economic rationale for replacing agents with robots. Since the average customer service agent wage of $34,164 (€29,552), as of April 29, 2018,[108] is relatively low compared to other areas with highly paid workers, such as accounting and fraud management, businesses are focusing their transformation projects elsewhere.

106 McKinsey Quarterly, 2016
107 McKinsey Quarlerly, 2016
108 "Customer Service Representative Salaries," 2018

However, while customer service jobs are generally low-skilled, there are a whole lot of them, operating at contact centers in generally low-profit or loss-making customer service departments with increasing economical pressure. Only a 5% decrease of customer service jobs in an industry employing 2.5 million workers in the U.S. alone can lead to $4.3 billion in savings. So, how can customer service agents save their jobs? Be human!

## ▌ Make a joke, be creative and use empathy!

Any tasks requiring creative and social intelligence make your job less susceptible to automation.[109] The psychological process underlying human creativity is difficult to quantify, so it's difficult for computers to reproduce. According to Boden[110] creativity is the ability to come up with ideas that are novel and valuable. Have you ever cracked a joke that you just kind of made up based on the situation you found yourself in? That's creative intelligence in its best form. For a computer to make a subtle joke, it would require a database with a vast knowledge comparable to that of a human. Moreover, the computer would need to be taught all the relevant methods of benchmarking the appropriate level of subtlety that it could use to create a joke that's funny without at the same time being offensive or awkward.

Human social intelligence is important in a wide range of customer service-related tasks, such as those involving negotiation, persuasion and care. To aid the computerization

109 Frey and Osborne, 2013
110 Boden, 2003

of such tasks, active research is being undertaken within the fields of Affective Computing[111] and Social Robotics.[112] However, the effective use of emotions by computers is still far behind human capabilities. Although computers are increasingly capable of detecting and identifying human emotions with advanced speech analytics, text-sentiment analysis and facial-impression-detecting algorithms, they generally fail in responding to emotions in a human-like way.

> **The use of emotions by computers is still far behind human capabilities.**

Since 1990, the Loebner Prize, an annual Turing test competition, awards prizes to human-like textual chat programs. Sophisticated algorithms have so far failed to convince judges. If you're a customer service agent or manager, using your emotions is one of the best ways to keep your job. Just try to use the right emotions at the right time. As many customers would surely confirm, it's better to speak with a cold-hearted computer than a rude and disrespectful human agent. Let's look at some other ways to guard yourself against automation.

111  Pickard, 2000
112  Ge, 2017

# CONTINUOUSLY IMPROVE YOUR PRODUCTIVITY

Improving your individual productivity at work decreases the chances that your role will be replaced by a computer. For obvious reasons, employers prefer to replace workers whose productivity stagnates or decreases over time. Research shows there are five key factors that fundamentally affect individual work productivity.

**FIVE KEY FACTORS TO IMPROVE YOUR PRODUCTIVITY**

1. **Connect and engage**: Productivity improves by 20-25% in organizations with connected employees.[113] You can connect with Slack, email, internal discussion forums, or simply "like" a cool post on the company Facebook page from time to time. Be part of the company you work for. Speak up when you dislike something, and be responsive to questions and requests for help from others.[114] Moreover, teams with high employee engagement rates are 21% more productive and have 28% less internal theft than those with low engagement.[115] Being engaged is good for both the employee and the company.

---

113 Chui, et. al., 2012
114 Chui, et. al., 2012
115 Dvorak and Cruse, 2016

2. **Use your strengths**: Employees who exercise their strengths on a daily basis are 8% more productive and 6x more likely to be engaged.[116] Identify what you're great at and what makes you special. Then do it every day. Trying to improve all your weaknesses is waste of time, as someone will always be better at things that don't come naturally to you. Focus instead on perfecting what makes you special. Good at presenting? Become the best pitch-maker in your company! Good at organizing internal contests? Organize the company Olympic games and rewrite company history!

3. **Stay loyal**: High-performing employees have three things in common: talent, high engagement, and 10+ years of service within the company.[117] Loyalty to an employer pays off, which is why it's so important to choose the company you work for wisely. Because leaving after a year or three might make you more experienced on the market, but you lose invaluable company-specific knowledge. Being the guy who "knows it all" and who "went through all the ups and downs" in the past with the company makes you special, and as research shows, also more productive.

116 Flade et. al., 2015
117 Harter, 2015

4. **Increase your focus**: 40% of workers feel overwhelmed by information, 27% by technology, and six in 10 workers believe that work overload is most harmful to their productivity.[118] If you're reading this chapter while holding a buzzing smartphone in one hand and a cup of coffee in the other, listening to a CNN broadcast on the screen in front of you and occasionally talking to colleagues, you are certainly addicted to multi-tasking. Face it, the computer sitting at your desk has already been able to multi-task much better than you for some time, and you're not going to beat it. Focusing on one task at a time actually makes you more productive, which fundamentally increases your value.

5. **Manage your time**: Work overload decreases productivity in 68% of employees, who feel they don't have enough hours in the day to complete their tasks.[119] Do you really know anyone from work who hasn't felt burned out at some point in their career? Burning out in a job is a very unpleasant state of mind that's preceded by a long period of being "too busy," working extra hours, losing sleep and family time and forsaking friends to meet aggressive deadlines. While giving "110%" for a few days in order to finish an important project might make you feel like Superman once you finish, no one can be Superman all the time. Except maybe Superman, but let's face it, he isn't going to be replaced by AI anytime soon, unless the Terminator thinks otherwise!

118 "State of the Workplace Report 2014," 2014
119 Sanders, G.I., 2017

# A GUIDE FOR MAKING YOUR JOB IRREPLACEABLE

This chapter has already mentioned that most existing job roles can be replaced by automation to some extent. Moreover, you read that currently used technologies enable the automation of any work task, assuming enough data is available. So your job is most likely in danger. No matter whether you are a customer service rep responding to hundreds of customers every day, a team leader managing others, or a director with responsibility for part of the business, your job will most likely fundamentally change in the coming decades. And in order for you to remain a valuable part of the business world and make a decent living, you need to change as well.

## CHECKLIST OF AN IRREPLACEABLE CUSTOMER SERVICE WORKER

By analyzing research on the future of work, computer automation and human labor, I've created a list of 10 key personal work attributes to help make your job irreplaceable. If you apply at least seven of the following 10 attributes in your day-to-day work, the probability of your job being replaced by a computer is significantly reduced, if not eliminated entirely. However, it's important to note that this research is based on currently available technological capabilities, and due to the anticipated rapid improvement of computational technology in the near future, the situation is very likely to change.

### 1. You leverage social skills and social intelligence in human interactions

O Front-line agents: Are you in frequent contact with customers?

O Using your emotions and intuition: Are you empowered to use your emotions (laughter, expressions of sadness and understanding) in communication with colleagues and customers? Are you ever praised for using your intuition at work?

### 2. You apply industry expertise

O Using your expertise beyond defined scripts: Are you empowered to use your own judgement and expertise?

O Actively working on creating new solutions by using your creativity: Do you use your own creativity to find new solutions in every job?

O Active participation in decision-making and planning: Are you part of decision-making and planning activities within your company?

### 3. You are continuously learning
O Do you learn something new every week that you put into practice at work?
O Do you attend training sessions on new techniques, expertise and processes at least once a month?

### 4. You are engaged and connected to peers
O Do you use internal company chat and social media groups, or do you interact with your work peers on a daily basis?

### 5. You utilize personal strengths
O Do you know your strengths that are relevant to your job?
O Do you use your strengths in your daily job?

### 6. You are continuously seeking new problems to solve
O Do you join and actively work to solve new problems, participating in new solutions, campaigns and product offerings, occasionally joining new initiatives and company activities?
O Do you expand or change your role within the company occasionally? Embrace change, as the unpredictability brought by new problems minimizes the chances of job being replaced by automation.
O Do you work in an unpredictable physical environment defined by many movements, logistical changes, etc.?

**7. You have optimized task management and you're not overworked**

O Do you frequently use workforce optimization systems, task management tools, project management tools or ticketing systems in order to maximize your productivity?

O Do you meet your realistically set individual goals and targets to avoid overworking?

O Are you part of an agile team working frequently to solve new problems and to come up with fast solutions?

**8. You use minimal data and technologies with maximum relevancy**

O Do you work in an environment with as few software interfaces as possible?

O Do you use only data that's necessary for conducting tasks in a meaningful and efficient way without getting overwhelmed?

**9. You are a long-term employee**

O Do you improve your productivity by leveraging knowledge, expertise and inter-personal relationship gained over time?

O Are you an active contributor to company culture?

**10. You manage others**

O Are you a team leader, manager or senior expert with coaching or mentoring responsibilities?

These 10 personal attributes are key stepping stones to ensuring your continued relevance at work. How do you add up? If there are elements you're missing, consider expanding your job to include the missing activities. Not only will this improve your standing and expertise at work, it will help ensure that your job won't be taken over by a computer any time soon.

# CHAPTER SUMMARY

Customer service industry, employing over 14M workers will be fundamentally changed due to automation, artificial intelligence and overall technological advancement in the upcoming decades. Automation will affect portions of almost every job to some degree and create new jobs that do not exist now. Customer service professionals who train or manage other team members are less likely to see their job fundamentally transformed in the near future. Customer service agents are recommended to continuously learn and work on increasing productivity and utilising emotional intelligence, empathy and expert skills and knowledge to develop their careers.

CHAPTER 5

# THE NEW AND LIBERATED AGENT

The previous chapter looked at the exciting ways that automation and technology is already integrating with today's style of working. It also looked at how we can ensure that humans remain relevant as employees in the face of increasing automation. So what will the customer service agent of the future look like? Well, to a certain extent the future is already here.

Meet Ivo, just another customer service rep. Actually, not really. Ivo is part of the new breed of Liberated Agents. He was born 27 years ago in Brno, a small Czech town near Austria. There is a majestic Gothic castle called Spilberk, built in the 13th century, on top of a hill overlooking a small city center that's now full of hipster coffee houses and bars.

27 years ago, there were none of these hipster baristas pouring perfect flat-whites made from home-roasted Kenya coffee beans. Ivo moved to Prague, the Czech capital, to pursue his studies in Marketing after he finished high school. Soon he joined an international telecommunications company to learn the ropes and earn some money. For him, like for many people around the world, the first job available at a large consumer-focused corporation was a call center representative. It's a daily drill: come to a large open-space office by 7 am, put on your headset, click the "available now" button on the computer screen and there you go, the first call is coming in.

It was probably the rare combination of great communication skills, a give-a-damn and make-it-happen attitude, and a self-imposed drive to pursue his career in Marketing that got Ivo promoted from his position as a contact center rep picking up phones to a member of a new, highly selective team of Social Customer Service Agents. They were a team of just seven, all between 23 and 30 years old and all with limited call center experience, but with a smartphone always in the palm of their hands ready to check Facebook or take a picture and post it on Instagram, and constantly getting global news notifications from the CNN mobile app while watching DVTV (a local digital TV news station delivering 20-minute interviews with the local political and social elite) while sitting in the bathroom. Doesn't sound like that typical call center agent we talked about earlier, right?

Ivo speaks to hundreds of customers every day. Those customers post their questions and complaints on the company Facebook page, their Twitter channel, and their Instagram and Youtube accounts. His responses – informative, structured, tailor-made to the customer and often enriched with an animated GIF to make the customer laugh when her request has been resolved – are seen by thousands of customers on a daily basis. His words are constantly watched by other Facebook users and occasionally liked when he nails a perfect response to a really angry customer and turns her into a calm (from what you can judge from a Facebook post) customer who's no longer ready to jump ship in just a few minutes.

The company Twitter profile, which is dedicated to sharing marketing messages and resolving customer service requests, gets hundreds of new followers every day. Why do people follow a channel like that? Don't they have more fun channels to follow? How can a telco operator compete with half-naked pictures of a heavily tattooed Justin Bieber, or the razor-sharp mouth of the current President of the United States, or the world-saving status updates of Bill Gates? It can't. But many customers (and perhaps many people who are not customers and just follow for fun, also known as "future customers") have received fast, simple, yet effective and friendly customer service from a guy named Ivo. So, by living through this short encounter with a surprisingly friendly young guy representing a global corporation, they become followers of an otherwise fairly boring multinational telecommunications giant with 15 management layers between the consumer and the CEO, a rigid German management style and shareholders eager to see 3%+ returns on their investments announced on quarterly shareholder calls.

Ivo. The Agent Liberated. Ivo is the man. And there are others like him. Six others in his team, to be exact. And a few hundred more in the Czech Republic working for other multinational corporations and quickly expanding startups. Plus there are thousands in Europe and hundreds of thousands around the world, responding to your Facebook request to upgrade your seat on the afternoon flight, resolving your failed repurchase of a mobile data package on your iPhone, or checking the availability of the new Beats headphones with a local retailer. They want the same thing as Aaran. They want to make customers happy (read: loyal, upselling and cross-selling) while being efficient (read: costing the company as little as possible). But somehow you feel that Aaran and Ivo are not the same at all. So what is it that makes them different?

Let's start with the basics. Ivo is probably a bit like you, a social and mobile customer. He lives in a city near you, he got a similar education; in fact, he might have attended the very same school as you. He has the same or similar hobbies and quite possibly listens to the same bands on Spotify as you do. Ivo has very similar beliefs as you do, he behaves based on the same values and cultural norms, and he goes for drinks with friends that are a lot like yours. Moreover, the same smartphone is buzzing in his pocket, the same laptop is hidden in the computer pocket in his stylish Timbuk2 backpack on his shoulders and he likes, shares and retweets quite similar content as you do on Facebook, Twitter and other social sites. Ivo is like you. In fact, Ivo might be you.

Aaran might be you too. But the chances are considerably lower. Unless you were born in India, raised in India and work in India, there aren't many things you have in common. Born to a different culture, raised within a different environment, having friends you've never known, listening to music you've never heard of and watching Bollywood movies your local theater doesn't run. What you have in common with Aaran for sure is the same telephone line. Your call reaches him in desperate times when something goes wrong and you need help from a customer service advisor. But as much as Aaran would like to help you, his chances of making himself relevant and helpful to you is nearly impossible. In fact, a computer bot using the most advanced technology currently available is likely to be better than him in many respects.

Now let's talk money. What puts Aaran and Ivo on the same page is that they both get a decent salary for their jobs. Ivo's annual salary of 346,000 Czech Crowns ($16,000, €13,840)[120] can buy him 4,108 Big Macs, while Aaran's annual salary of $3,000 (€2,595) will buy him only 1,063 Big Macs.[121]

120 Platy.cz, 2018
121 "The Big Mac Index," 2018

That's still a lot of Big Macs, but it's more than three times less than what Ivo can buy for his money in the country where he lives. Aaran's living conditions have improved over the recent decades, but it's still either impossible or very challenging for him to get a good education, travel the world and see the world from a similar perspective as those customers calling him from different countries.

Ivo is an eager social media user, frequently posting pictures and sharing videos on Facebook, adding #foodporn pictures on Instagram, occasionally retweeting Kanye West on Twitter and watching music videos on YouTube every day. Ivo also creates and manages a lot of pages and events on social media and his parents call him a "tech geek." Although he likes to play with technology, he really loves working in marketing because he gets to help brands build relationships with customers through emotion, understanding and dialogue. Conversation over monologue. Service over advertisement. Satisfaction over productivity.

Ivo and Aaran will probably never meet. But you can easily meet both of them. Tweeting your customer service question will lead you to Ivo, while calling a 1-800 number will probably connect you to Aaran. The question is what Aaran will do when nobody calls him anymore.

Earlier this year, Ivo left his job in the contact center. He is now managing the brand of a mobile operator across 12 countries and building strategies for engaging tens of millions of customers every day on social media. The phone-handling contact center rep has become an international marketing manager. That's what the role of digital customer service advisor prepared him for.

# TOP TRAITS OF LIBERATED CUSTOMER SERVICE AGENTS

The following is a list of top traits to look for in customer service agents who are ready for new, transhuman digital customer service. It was developed with the team responsible for social customer service at T-Mobile Austria, the telecommunications company.

1. **Cosmopolitan**: Someone who knows what's going on in the world. They're interested in a little bit of everything, including gaming, network trends and even politics.
2. **Team player**: Teamwork is essential for a social care agent. The community is public and interacts in real-time. Everyone needs to pull together as a team.
3. **Authentic**: Just as there are different types of customers, there needs to be different types of agents. Be unique, smart and individual. Be you.
4. **Creative**: Social media, messengers and other digital channels have their own rulebooks and agents must find the right balance between standard procedures and doing what's best for the customer.
5. **Courageous**: Agents must have the confidence to engage with customers in real-time, on a public forum, with everyone watching.
6. **Patient**: Agents must take the necessary time for each customer. The aim is to resolve and build a relationship, not force customers to disengage.

7. **Resourceful**: Even if a customer asks for something beyond your control (ie., a broken printer) take a look at forums or just ask Google. It's about finding a solution together.
8. **Empathetic**: This core characteristic is evident in digital communication and the dedication an agent shows to connecting with and helping customers.
9. **Respectful**: Agents must never forget they are writing to a customer and must always demonstrate mutual respect and restraint from negative reactions.

Looking for these characteristics in new customer service agents will help prepare you for the evolution of digital customer service in the future. Let's take a closer look at the hiring process.

# HIRING TIPS FOR RECRUITING LIBERATED CUSTOMER SERVICE AGENTS

This collection of recommendations and tips for recruiting the best Liberated Agents was created for a case study by Brand Embassy, the customer service technology company, with Ivo Marecek, a consultant and former social media customer service leader at T-Mobile Group, the telecommunications company.[122] Yes, that same Ivo who inspired me to write this chapter about the new breed of customer service professionals.

**Start hiring inside your company**: The best job candidates probably already work in your company. They understand customer needs, how the company can help them and which internal processes lead to customer satisfaction.

**Find candidates active on social media**: Active social media users have learned what content is good and bad to share. They have also learned what tone of voice is optimal, how to approach large and small communities, and what formats and copy lengths work best to create an appropriate feedback loop. Moreover, active social media users (those who write and publish their own content and comment on the content of others, rather than simply sharing the content of others) are typically those who care about having their

122 Brand Embassy, 2018

voice heard, which is an important attribute of the work of customer service agents.

**Look for masters of the written word**: No, she will no longer be picking up phones. You are not looking for a great orator who knows all the tricks of how to use different accents to sound local. You are looking for a person who's great at typing, amazing at putting thoughts into easily understandable and engaging sentences, and who can summarize even complex problems into a "post-it" format.

**Uncover your company's innovators**: The traditional customer service job used to be very repetitive and boring, since most of the interactions were prescribed by company scripts and communication manuals. With an increasing number of repetitive jobs being automated, customer service agents are and will be even more focused on more complex issues, the solutions of which require creativity and innovative ideas. Look for creative people who always find a way where there has been no way before.

**Support your cross-departmental communicators**: Solving a complex issue requires leaving the comfortable office chair and knocking on a few office doors. Having good relationships across departments, being liked and popular throughout the company and knowing all the tips and tricks to get other people to help you is very important. Moreover, as you've read in earlier chapters, this is also a skill that is very hard to replace by automation.

**Develop people-centred people, not policy enforcers**: "Based on internal policy, dear customer, I'm not allowed to offer you any additional discount," says an unpopular customer service agent who will never be contacted by the customer again. "I'm so sorry, Paula, I've tried to request an even better price, but the 15% discount is the best we can do now. But I have found a way to add this product for free if you sign up for two years. What do you think?" says an agent you want to have on your team.

**Give your team room to be real**: There's a reason why you still hire human beings for a contact center, although many of their tasks can already be replaced by automation. They are real humans. And real human customers like to speak with real human agents. So give agents space to remain real, authentic personalities, and help them find out how their personality helps them to achieve their daily goals.

# CHAPTER SUMMARY

The best customer service agents on the market today exhibit traits that will continue to make them valuable in the future. These include a familiarity with social media and written communication skills. They are highly creative, empathetic and are not afraid to be authentic in communication with customers. Employers should give them a high degree of freedom and empower them to be efficient and passionate in working with colleagues internally as well as with customers.

# CHAPTER 6

# THE
# CHALLENGES

Customer service agents like Ivo, whom we met in the previous chapter, will continue to enjoy job security in the future because they'll continue to play an irreplaceably valuable role in building relationships between customers and brands. But fundamental technological innovations don't come without risks and challenges. Technology can malfunction or be wrongly designed, or people can misuse the technology. In this chapter, we will explore the challenges that need to be overcome and the threats that should be eliminated in order to fully realize the positive effects of transhuman customer service transformation.

# CUSTOMER DATA PROTECTION

Countries around the world are working furiously to prepare for the coming of AI because this technology has the potential to make sweeping change in both business and personal life. The question of security, for both individuals and companies, is very important. There have been recent occurrences of hacking attacks using advanced AI to penetrate customer or citizen data, with huge impacts in terms of commercial losses and brand equity.[123] There have also been numerous examples of personal data theft recently, including the proven Russian penetration and hijacking of Paypal accounts and over 100,000 real Facebook profiles to infiltrate the public discourse in the run-up to the 2016 US Presidential elections, all of which has been well-documented by The Wall Street Journal[124] among many others. Finally, there's the growing trend of personal data theft by using advanced AI technologies and automation services. All of these issues need to be addressed in the immediate future. Customer service is naturally working with sensitive customer data and therefore both employees and technology partners need to be properly trained, and policies and processes need to be set up in a way that minimizes potential data leakages.

123 Elazari, 2018
124 Seetharaman, 2017

# ECONOMICAL UNPREPAREDNESS

With all the potential economic devastation and benefit of AI, we have to ask: are the world's leading economies really prepared? "World Bank data has predicted that the proportion of jobs threatened by automation in India is 69 percent, 77 percent in China and as high as 85 percent in Ethiopia," according to World Bank President Jim Yong Kim in 2016.[125] It really does sound like we might be facing the end of work as we know it.

Many of these fears can be traced back to a 2013 study from the University of Oxford. This made a much-quoted prediction that 47% of jobs in the US were under threat of automation in the next two decades. Other more recent and detailed studies have made similar dramatic predictions. In 2017, Elon Musk, the CEO of Tesla Motors, SpaceX and a frequent AI commentator, told the National Governors Association that job disruption caused by technology was the scariest problem to him.[126] Musk and other entrepreneurs see a Universal Basic Income, or UBI, as one way to provide a buffer to give humans time to retrain themselves to do what robots can't. Some believe that it might even spawn a new wave of entrepreneurs, giving those displaced workers a shot at the American Dream. But UBI is complex, and we're nowhere near reaching a consensus. One of the biggest problems with UBI is that a base sum that would allow people to refuse

125 "69 Percent of Jobs in India Threatened by Automation: World Bank," 2016
126 Clifford, 2017

work and look for something better (rather than just allowing employers to pay workers less) is around $1,000 (€865) per month, which would cost most countries somewhere between five and 35 percent of their GDP.[127] But there are already interesting experiments taking place to see what can be done.

Sam Altman's experiment, named the Basic Income Project, will involve 3,000 people in two states over five years. Some 1,000 of them will be given $1,000 (€865) a month, and the rest will get just $50 (€43) a month and serve as a sort of control group. This project should reveal some important information about how people will behave when given free money, providing an evidence-based way to think about UBI—we don't have much of that evidence now. Among the questions hopefully to be answered: Will people use the cushion of free money to look for better work? Will they go back to school for retraining? Will the neurological development of children improve? Will crime rates go down? We will see. But the economy is only one part of this conundrum.

# ETHICAL CONCERNS

There are several ethical questions concerning transhumanism. The possibility of immortality is one of them. Was man made to be immortal, and is it morally permissible to make ourselves so? Do these questions even matter? It depends on your point of view, and perhaps your degree of religious feeling. But one thing is for certain: many

127 Ito, 2018

of the smartest people in the world have weighed in on the potentialities of AI, and they're not all convinced that it will be a good thing for society.

As Stephen Hawking said, "Success in creating effective AI, could be the biggest event in the history of our civilization. Or the worst. We just don't know. So we cannot know if we will be infinitely helped by AI, or ignored by it and side-lined, or conceivably destroyed by it. Unless we learn how to prepare for, and avoid, the potential risks, AI could be the worst event in the history of our civilization. It brings dangers, like powerful autonomous weapons, or new ways for the few to oppress the many. It could bring great disruption to our economy."[128]

We'll come back to the possible economic implications of AI, but for now it's important to consider that if a brilliant mind such as Hawking had reservations about AI, then perhaps that should pause. The fact is we just can't be sure of the future of AI until it's here. Hawking wasn't the only voice who has been less than enthusiastic about AI. Noam Chomsky is another prominent thinker who has been outspoken about the possible dangers of AI becoming another NSA (the US National Security Agency).[129]

So what's everybody worried about? Nothing less than the future, or the end, of human life on earth. As Bostrom has said, "we're like children playing with a bomb."[130] And that's an interesting connection to make because the ethical and societal questions we're facing with AI are in some ways similar to those that a previous generation faced with the

128 Kharpal, 2017
129 Chomsky, 2017
130 Bostrom, 2015

development of the atomic bomb. This was one of the most dramatic and painful moments in human history and in the development of technology. As J. Robert Oppenheimer, a scientist who was crucial in the development of the atom bomb, famously said when he witnessed the first test detonation, "Now I am become Death, the destroyer of worlds."[131] It's a quote from the Bhagavad Gita and it shows the ambivalence and doubt that plagued this project, and caused even the inventors of the bomb to wish they had not invented it. But much like the scientists who are today on the forefront of developing AI, Oppenheimer and his colleagues faced conflicting motivations, and they also faced the unknown because they were developing powerful technology that had never before been put to use. Like the atom bomb, AI has the potential to change the world, and society will never be the same once we unleash it. It is important to realize that unlike in the past, the influence on society of software engineers and mathematicians who create AI algorithms has dramatically increased. That's because a single piece of software or one algorithm can cause the death or serious harm of many.

A set of ethical norms and guidelines needs to be developed and largely accepted by the academic, political and business communities building the next AI technologies in order to avoid AI going bad or being misused. New algorithms making AI smarter and more capable should go through a detailed ethical review before they are published and more than a handful of other scientists can use them. I suspect that in the coming years, we are going to see

131 Temperton, 2017

more ethical discussions about the use of technology than ethical discussions concerning human behavior. Ethics and computers is likely to become a common topic in both popular and scientific papers.

> **Ever wondered about immortality? Mike More, the founder of the Humanity+ organization, an international nonprofit that advocates the ethical use of technology to expand human capacities, is also CEO of a company that performs cryonics, the preservation of human corpses in liquid nitrogen after legal death, in the hopes of restoring them to full health when hypothetical new technology is developed in the future. As of early 2017, Alcor had more than 1,136 members, including 317 associate members and 153 members in cryopreservation, as whole bodies or brains. Alcor also cryopreserves pets. By 2007, there were 33 animals preserved.[132]**

# TOO MUCH REGULATION

The recent advent of AI and its potential danger call for more regulation. But what is the right level of regulation that minimizes risks but still motivates meaningful innovation? No matter how you feel about the positive or negative possibilities of transhuman technologies, it's clear that more preparation is better. So the good news is that both the EU

132 "Membership and Applicant Growth," 2015

and the US are laying down laws to help regulate AI when it gets here in full force.

The European Union has been preparing for the advent of AI at least since 2015, when it issued the Declaration of Cooperation on Artificial Intelligence, which has been signed by 25 countries. This declaration is one of the world's most coordinated plans to deal with the advent of AI. It covers all the major bases, including technological, ethical, legal and socio-economic aspects. The idea is to get ahead of the curve, ensuring that the EU and its citizens can take advantage of this technology. In order to meet these goals, the European Commission is currently putting a lot of money into AI. In fact they are increasing yearly investments into AI by 70% under a project called Horizon 2020. Over the next couple years the investment will reach upwards of 1.5 billion euro.[133]

But the EU isn't only thinking about money. They're also making strides to ensure that AI is used to the advantage of citizens and businesses. Individual countries and the European Commission as a whole are currently working to attract AI talent, and to set up more areas for training and research into AI and its capabilities. Finally, the EU is also working on directives for the ethical use of AI.[134]

As one of the world leaders in business and technology, the US is planning to take advantage of the AI revolution too. They're putting together a comprehensive set of new regulations.[135] There has been a concerted effort to predict what the important issues will be with the advent of AI, and numerous governmental planning boards have already

133 "What Is Horizon 2020?," 2014.
134 "Artificial Intelligence," 2018
135 Chessen, 2017

started putting together ideas for regulations that cover all aspects of AI, spanning from job loss to data theft threats.

One example is the Ethics and Governance of Artificial Intelligence Fund. It's a project to support work that speeds up the development of ethical AI frameworks, specifically concerning applied research and education. The Berkman Klein Center, as well as Harvard and the MIT Media Lab have been at the forefront of this project.[136] The Association for the Advancement of Artificial Intelligence is another important group in this regard. They're a nonprofit scientific society that's working to advance the scientific understanding of the mechanisms underlying thought and intelligent behavior and their embodiment in machines.

But don't expect other countries to be left behind in terms of AI. China has committed to becoming the world AI Superpower in the $150 billion (€129 billion) industry, and they certainly have the money and the manpower to make that happen.[137] It's likely that AI will be the new space race, with superpowers competing to be the first to make important advancements in this powerful technology.

The leading technology firms have also recognized how important it is that their thoughts on the future of AI be taken into account. Microsoft, Google, Facebook, Amazon and IBM set up The Partnership on AI in 2016[138] to study and formulate the best practices for the ethical use of AI.

Most of these regulations are for the good, however there is the possibility that further laws and regulations might affect the speed of AI implementation for commercial

136 "AI Fund FAQ," 2006.
137 Ferreira, 2018
138 You can learn more at www.partnershiponai.org

use. One of the dangers of governments overstepping their regulatory roles are new laws that would direct AI research to specific fields of expertise or for specific use cases. Scientists and innovative companies should be left to work freely on any innovation they consider meaningful. Another challenge might come from new regulations that are influenced by partisan political views. Instead, new regulations concerning AI should be designed with a long-term view of the possible impacts on society in many generations to come. The academic world, businesses both small and large and the general public should be interested in new regulations being developed and should engage in dialogue supporting the introduction of a minimal level of continuously updated regulation.

# EMPLOYEE PROTECTION LAWS

The story of Queen Elizabeth II destroying plans for a more efficient knitting machine mentioned earlier in this book shows how rapid technological innovation sometimes get slowed down by political short-termism. Take another example mentioned earlier, of Uber potentially replacing millions of professional drivers with autonomous cars. When the jobs of millions of voters are at stake, the long-term rationale for higher general well-being is easily forgotten. We can expect that politicians will try to ratify bills ensuring minimal human labor contributions to products being manufactured or services being provided in order to make sure that robots will not take over certain industries completely. This is, in the long-term, equally harmful for consumers, workers and businesses. Employees need some time to re-skill and re-train themselves to find their irreplaceable value on the job market, but laws should not step into this organic trend as it can cause more harm than good. For example, countries not implementing such laws could take advantage of the situation and we could see another massive off-shoring trend, this time for reasons that don't have to do with the economy. It is the opinion of the author that new laws should be implemented in order to continually increase the minimum wage and motivate both employers and employees to invest much more time and money into education, re-skilling and training.

The companies that introduce new automation that could potentially make some employees redundant should focus on employee development programs or proactive communication with employees. It's important to explain the reasons that new innovations are being implemented, how the new hardware or software will make human jobs more meaningful and valuable, and what opportunities are available to the employees to grow within their job roles.

# BRAND REPUTATION LOSS

Have you heard the story of the chatbot called Tay who went rogue? By 2016, Microsoft had developed its flagship AI-powered chatbot they said could teach itself to have a dialogue with any human. Only hours later it was using one bad word after another, having been inspired by creative Twitter users trying to explore how smart the technology was. It didn't take long before Tay started to spread racial and genocidal comments, causing Microsoft executives unexpected troubles and generating an international PR blunder for one of the biggest companies in the world.[139] This and many other stories that pop up in daily newspapers and online blogs every now and then show how incomplete, poorly tested products may easily cause significant damage to brand equity and company investors.

How can companies avoid causing unnecessary troubles to their brand reputation? It helps to first set appropriate public expectations from anticipated new product releases. Some technology companies first launch products internally to fix the most pressing bugs, then continue with Alpha releases to early adopters and testing groups before publishing the product in Beta for the general public while still keeping expectations low by emphasising that it's a product in the early stage of development. Moreover, some companies first focus new products on rather small customer segments to test how well they are received before tackling the mass market. Human supervision is also very important: it takes only a few minutes for an autonomous software using natural language processing and machine learning to pick up bad habits from their test users and it takes only one or two tweets to case a public outrage. That's why AI companies increasingly hire "Chief AI Safety Officers" to serve as a kill switch for potential threats caused by the development of new technology.

139 Price, 2016

# CUSTOMER DISSATISFACTION

Do you know what's worse than an old-fashioned IVR system making you "press one to get recent offers" when you just want to speak with a friendly advisor? It's the same dumb IVR system doing the same thing with Facebook Messenger or WhatsApp to serve you the annoying options. Why? Because customers have much higher expectations from engaging with brands over new channels such as messengers compared to traditional phone calls. And yet, there are plenty of companies launching fairly simple-minded chatbots that cause customer frustrations every day. Every chatbot or piece of Artificial Intelligence technology companies develop should be at least 10 times better than their existing solution. That's the "10x Rule" that helped Google and other leading companies get to their market positions. Moreover, as you learned earlier in this book, negative customer emotions are typically caused by a complete lack of response, a slow response or missed expectations. Focusing on the value that will be delivered by providing faster, more efficient customer care is more important than being the first on the market to launch a chatbot or Intelligent Advisor.

# PUBLIC DISBELIEF

Misleading newspaper titles such as "'Killer robots': AI experts call for boycott over lab at South Korea university"[140] or "Doomsday AI will cause a nuclear war by 2040 that could DESTROY humanity"[141] may cause the progress of innovation in transhuman technologies to significantly slow down in the coming years. Why? Non-educated journalists seeking clickbait rather than well-researched stories exaggerate what the current technologies can actually do. This makes the public (and some politicians who use the press as their main research source) believe that we are already on the verge of singularity where computers will take over most of what humans do in their daily lives. Facing the reality that we are decades from that point, or that we might not reach that point during our lifetimes, makes people believe less in current progress so the media and politicians move onto other popular topics. This trend isn't happening for the first time. The so-called "AI Winter" followed a similar story arc in the 1980s when the public generally believed that under-developed hardware could handle technologies surpassing human intelligence and that AI algorithms could make better decisions than humans. They could not, and in the following years an industry worth a billion dollars practically disappeared.[142]

We could soon be facing another AI winter. If companies fail to live up to high expectations of AI driving safely autonomous cars or Intelligent Advisors chatting with

140 Haas, 2018.
141 Collins, 2018.
142 Crevier, 1993

humans over the phone, another wave of disbelief in technological progress could take place. In order to avoid this situation, scientists and innovative companies should manage public expectations and journalists should educate themselves and provide more holistic and well-balanced stories. The general public is right to get excited (and worried too) about what's coming, but we should be cautious. Much of the technology we're talking about should be considered a future possibility rather than a foregone conclusion. Keep that in mind the next time you read another bombastic news headline.

# CHAPTER SUMMARY

Companies need to comply with new customer data protection regulations and they need to invest more to protect customer data. Moreover, employers need to invest into employee development programs and proactive communication with employees and customers when implementing new automation initiatives to avoid employee or customer dissatisfaction and loss of brand equity. Governments need to avoid introducing unnecessary employee protection regulations that slow down the meaningful innovation of technology. Finally, the media and the general public should avoid publishing and believing, respectively, bombastic news headlines about the possibilities of AI that are yet to be realized. This will help us avoid another "AI Winter."

# CHAPTER 7

# MY VISION OF WHAT'S COMING

Imagine for a minute you've never heard about underpaid Aaran in his offshore New Delhi call center and that you've never had to deal with unhelpful, idiotic voice robots when calling your bank's customer service hotline. Imagine that the customer service of the future is amazing, full of mind-blowing technological innovations connected to the deep understanding of customer emotions and needs. Imagine that a call center isn't a cheap open-space building on the outskirts of a rural region with low salaries, but a shiny, hip building in downtown Brooklyn, or a cool new skyscraper designed by Zaha Hadid at Canary Wharf, the futuristic financial district of London. The customer service reps entering the building during morning rush hour are young, dynamic people wearing Supreme hats and New Balance sneakers, with the newest Google Chromebook laptops in their hands and iPhones buzzing in their pockets.

Imagine that the IT department of this contact center isn't full of 10-year-old PC computers and shelves stuffed with CD-ROM backups of outdated operating systems, but instead there are futuristic spaces with just a few servers for internal data and plenty of DevOps engineers on the line with Amazon Web Services experts, or talking with specialists from IBM Watson about the newest update to their AI search mechanisms, and having meetings in conference rooms with glass ceilings and cool sofas where they sit down with Oculus VR experts every Tuesday morning to talk about the newest developments of their virtual reality goggles, which enable shared 3D experiences with customers. Sounds too good to be true? You may be imagining the contact center of the future.

Let's take a look at some of the newest capabilities this contact center might have at their disposal.

# TELEPATHY

I know what you're thinking. Telepathy, really? Most of us found The Minority Report a little far-fetched. In the movie, precogs, or mutated humans, could predict murders before they happened by telepathically connecting to the minds of the murderers as they were about to pull out their Smith & Wesson and enter the house where their wife was having a good time with a person she definitely wasn't married to. Telepathy is something we've heard about from shady mind-readers asking for a few dollars before they read our partner's mind on the street. Telepathy is impossible. Right?

But what if it actually were possible? What if we could achieve telepathy through science? Our brain has a memory and processing power that's somewhat comparable to a computer. We store knowledge in the part of our brain called the limbic system, we store emotions and make decisions in the part called the amygdala. Our brain functions due to continuous caloric intake, and information from our brain is transferred into our movements, speech and thoughts by electrical transfers known as the firing of motor neurones. Compared to computers, we are like a MacBook Pro by the time we're 10 years old: highly capable, always evolving, incredibly powerful and, in most cases, not very buggy.

Telepathy, a term that comes from the Greek τῆλε, or tele, meaning "distant," and πάθος, pathos or patheia meaning "feeling or experience," is the purported transmission of information from one person to another without using any of our known sensory channels or physical interactions. In the customer service world this means that no telephone number needs to be dialed, no chat window needs to be opened, and no email message needs to be typed on the computer keyboard in order to satisfy a customer with an urgent request.

> **Humans are highly capable, always evolving, incredibly powerful and, in most cases, not very buggy.**

In April 2017, Mark Zuckerberg, the founder and CEO of Facebook, announced that the company is working on mind-reading technology. How awesome would it be if we could share Facebook updates just by thinking them? Sounds very cool, right? Oh wait, what if it also shared what I thought about that pretty lady walking past the coffeeshop where I'm sitting? And what if it also shared what I'm thinking about my boss? Hold your horses and read on. At Facebook's annual developer conference, Regina Dugan, head of the company's experimental technologies division Building 8, said Facebook was working on "optical neuro-imaging systems" that would allow people to type words directly from their brain at 100 words per minute: five times the speed possible on a smartphone.[143] This is probably very far from reaching the full potential of scientific telepathic communication, considering that a professional typewriter can type between 65 and 75 words per minute, but it's certainly real progress and a potentially life-changing innovation for people with disabilities.

How far we are from the day when we'll telepathically share a technical difficulty on our PC with an expert customer service rep without lengthy explanatory emails, several escalations and call transfers? Well, recent experiments

143 Constine, 2017

suggest that day is still a while in the future. In 2004, scientists from the Barcelona-based research institute Starlab, the French firm Axilum Robotics and Harvard Medical School ran an experiment in which Person A was supposed to make Person B say what Person A was thinking. Although this experiment proved successful and international media published articles promising an upcoming revolution in mind-sharing and telepathy, all the experiment succeeded in doing was transferring one word, "halo," to the other person in 70 minutes. That means it would take you 200 hours of brain-intensive telepathic activity to tell someone about your customer service problem!

One thing to consider about these experiments is that they've used off-the-shelf equipment that requires no surgery. The brain-reading part generally consists of putting a little cap of electrodes on someone's head. It's temporary. And it's painless.

Elon Musk recently invested into and became the CEO of a company called Neuralink only a few months after the company announced that telepathy technology would be available in the next few years. The 36,400-word-long illustrated explanation published in cooperation with the famous blogger and illustrator Tim Urban was supposed to explain how Neuralink will work. But the text missed several key details, so we need telepathic abilities to know how Elon will deliver what he's promised. Let's hope that his prediction will be delivered in a more timely fashion than the Tesla Model 3, which has over 400,000 customers impatiently waiting for their revolutionary electric car to be delivered as I write these lines, and learning every few weeks that their delivery is likely to be delayed by many more months.[144] You can be sure about one thing. Telepathy as a scientific method of communicating through technological progress is among the top priorities of the world's leading investors and entrepreneurs, and billions of dollars will be invested into this field very shortly in order to deliver real results as soon as possible.

By accepting this notion as a hypothesis that telepathy and other groundbreaking innovations will be technically possible in the foreseeable future, let's take our imagination on a journey into the contact center of the future. How will telepathy, superintelligent computers and brain implants be used by Ivo and other Liberated Agents who are eager to jump on another incoming request from a social and mobile customer?

# REWIND AND SHARE

Apple recently released the new iOS operating system for mobile phones and tablets. I installed the new update and since then my life has become significantly more filled with colorful language. Not only has my iPad became slower and more clunky, but many applications stopped working completely and required an update. An update that couldn't be downloaded since my iTunes account switched to an old account I no longer use which is associated with a credit card issued in a country I no longer live in. Since I couldn't update many of my communication apps, I lost track of

144 Regalado, 2017

some conversations with my colleagues and friends, which caused more problems. See how one mistake causing another creates a whole new chain of problems? Now imagine me explaining this to an Apple customer service rep in an email trail. Writing this chapter takes less time than explaining every detail and possibility about why this all went wrong. So many inter-dependencies and so many small errors connect to create one huge disappointing and nerve-wracking experience.

Now imagine that all this could go away and everything could start over with a single tap on the touch-screen in your hands. The button on the screen says "Rewind and Share," and what it does is actually very simple. It creates a copy of the recording of the experience your memory stored while you were having these problems, with every detail and thought process that went along with it, and shares this digital file with the responsible customer service agent with a simple message: "Please resolve now."

Mind-reading that enables customer service agents to rewind a past experience through the eyes of the customer is something you might have seen in the futuristic TV series Black Mirror, but the recent proclamations of leading scientists and entrepreneurs actually show that we aren't necessarily too far away from experiencing this ourselves.

# KNOW-IT-ALL MIKE

Do you remember "Know-it-all Mike"? That guy you met when you went to a local bank eager to open up a new account and ask about the optimal financial plan for your future? Mike, the banking advisor, knew it all. Or maybe your Mike had a different name. Maybe he was the type of "smart ass" that didn't listen to a word you were saying, who interrupted you in the middle of every other sentence with some "Yeah, I totally know what you mean" kind of comment without having a clue what you were talking about. Top that off with his 10-minute monologue about how to build a 100%-guaranteed bright financial future for you and your family, which had nothing to do with the reality of your life! Well, every bank has its Mike. Every contact center has several Mikes of their own, and you can bet you'll meet one soon if you haven't already had the pleasure.

But what if Mike really did know everything? What if he knew exactly what all other customer service reps and financial consultants know? Not individually, but all together. Mike, a customer service guy with the collected knowledge of every customer service issue ever recorded by the company, with every detail of every product offering, with absolute knowledge about the needs of the customers... impossible, right? Customer service agents get knowledge through onboarding, continuous internal trainings, occasional peer-to-peer consultations with colleagues, and access to a large spreadsheet of the most frequent customer requests and resolutions stored on his or her work station. This knowledge is very limited, every agent remembers something else, and therefore their approach and quality of service is different. More importantly, their knowledge is lost for the company and its customers when they leave their jobs.

Next time you meet Mike, he will actually be very helpful. He will provide you with accurate and exhaustive insights into your financial options and explain step-by-step how to open a bank account that's appropriate for you and your family, taking into account your actual preferences and expectations. Why? Because he's wearing a hat with digital transmitters that can transfer a collected knowledge base into his brain in real-time. Does that sound unrealistic?

Even today, you can download the Google Goggles app to your smartphone, point the camera at a building in front you and get a detailed description of the history of the building, a calendar of upcoming events happening in the basement club and contact details for the companies with offices on the upper floors. And Google Glass enables you to display all this information in front of your eyes like you were imagining it in your brain. Although we're talking about the very early stage of technological advancement in this area, the speed of development toward transferring large sums of data right into your brain, without the necessity of slowing down to read, to search or to ask a colleague, is increasing every year. The very near future will see chip implants in the brain or hats connected to an online knowledge base that enables the in-store agent to use all the collective wisdom of all agents in real-time while responding to a customer.

# "I KNOW HOW YOU FEEL."

Emotions drive most of the decisions in our lives. As we learned in previous chapters, many of the decisions we think we make rationally are in fact driven by our emotions and feelings. Name one occasion when you dealt with customer service and you weren't emotional. When something goes wrong or stops working, it's always at the worst possible time. Your adrenaline kicks in, you immediately feel the urge to fix it, to get it done, and you forget about everything else. And then your phone reaches the endless line of "valued customers who have called before you," or your email is responded to by an unhelpful service rep with zero understanding of what you need. So you explode. Enough! Just sort it out now and leave me alone!

The longest-lasting emotions are sadness, hope and joy.[145] When you feel sad or angry, you store this experience in your unconsciousness over the long-term, and there is a chance that the decision you make about your next purchase of a new smartphone or new shoes will be influenced by how you feel about the brand from a long time ago.

Are customer service agents trained to respond to emotions? Yes, but only to a very limited extent. In many of today's contact centers you might see a sticker reminding agents to "Show no emotions. Stay objective." Is behaving like a robot with no emotions really the best approach for making a sad customer happy again? I don't think so. Responding to a sad customer requires a different approach than responding to an angry individual. But understanding

145 Swinscoe, 2014

and correctly translating emotions into actions is very difficult. Assessing the level of sadness of a customer who tweeted a complaint in 140 characters, or an impatient customer who connected to a video chat for one minute, is difficult for humans. For technology it doesn't have to be. There are AI-powered emotion-identifying services already available on the market that assess customer emotions based on a semantic analysis of text, facial analysis on video or voice analysis on an incoming phone call. By improving the accuracy and quality of these services through more capable Artificial Intelligence, and by using the analysis to recommend the right actions to customer service agents, companies can significantly improve customer satisfaction.

So next time you contact customer support, an agent will see the moment she gets your "ticket" assigned how angry, sad, or curious you are. Then she'll be advised about the right tone of voice and approach to make you happy again.

# TYPING WITH 100 FINGERS

It's a Bot! They are using a robot to respond to my question! Maybe you've thought this when you just described a pretty complex issue you've had with the boiler in your apartment. The heat goes up and down, you get cold feet in the morning and you sweat all night. The thermostat has a mind of its own! So you spend 10 minutes describing the issue in a series of live chat messages to an agent named Amy. And only a few seconds after you hit the send button and share your complaint with her, Amy provides you with an incredibly accurate, custom-made step-by-step process for resolving the problem.

You'd think they've had this problem with tons of customers. But actually, you're the very first customer to experience this rather "edge case" of the product malfunctioning, and no pre-defined answer for Amy was suggested by the internal knowledge base system. So Amy wrote it up, character by character, word by word, sentence by sentence, and she sent you an exhaustive 300-word response in 10 seconds. How? Amy, a real human being sitting in a room surrounded by other human agents, didn't use her fingers to type you a response at 60 words per minute. Her computer automatically recorded her thoughts through chips attached to her head. She thought the response and it was instantly translated into text and sent to you. Typing is so old fashioned! With mind-reading and AI, you can write at the speed of your thoughts.

# UPLOADING KNOWLEDGE

"Tap here to upload your daily knowledge" says the futuristic flat screen on a desk in the living room. The computer turns on by 9 am every morning from Monday to Friday and goes into sleep mode six hours later. You'll notice all the game icons and educational apps on the home screen. There's also one for a customer service platform. Amy, a mother of three working as a home-based customer service agent for Amazon, turns on the customer service app every day as soon as she gets back from dropping off her kids at school.

She is one of tens of thousands of home-based customer service agents working for companies large and small around the world.

Since Amy works from home, she avoids two hours of commuting every day, which has allowed her to go back to work while raising three children. Customer service is ideal for her: she engages with people every day, turning their dissatisfaction into happiness, and uses the communication skills she's always prided herself on. All from the comfort of her apartment in the beautiful town of Scituate, Massachusetts.

One of the difficulties for customer service organizations that employ home-based agents is knowledge sharing and continuous education. Agents use their desktops to access knowledge bases built to choose the optimal resolution for a customer service issue, and they frequently use scripted texts defined centrally by the client to ensure a standardized tone of voice and quality of service. Although this might make sense from the corporate perspective, it sometimes makes Amy feel undervalued. "I know exactly what this nice old lady needs. I've had three other customers with similar problems over the past month. But the software I'm using seems to ignore this, and I'm getting misleading scripts to play with. It's frustrating!" It's hard for companies to gain individual knowledge of their front-level customer-facing agents, since they don't share an open-plan office with team leaders wandering among the desks and consulting on difficult situations. Instead, they're connecting from thousands of living rooms and home offices around the country.

What if there was a way to gather all the valuable knowledge agents gain every day? What if the company could provide updated scripts and case recommendations by 6 am every morning? What if this could all be done without a single person filling out a lengthy form, or analyzing thousands of hours of phone call recordings?

Sometimes also called Whole Brain Emulation (WBE), brain uploading or mind copying is the process of scanning the mental state of a particular brain substrate and copying it to a computer. Although today still in a theoretical stage of development, its use for customer service and employee knowledge sharing is undeniable. Ray Kurzweil, Director of Engineering at Google, reckons that people will be able to upload their brains and become "digitally immortal" by 2045.[146]

"Tap here to upload your daily knowledge." Amy confirms by tapping her touchscreen, and her experiences solving the case of the poor old lady, along with 50 other cases, transfers through tiny chips strapped to a somewhat funny looking hat she wears during her shift. The data uploads to the central database of the customer service platform, where it is analyzed automatically through machine learning, and anonymously and securely shared to thousands of agents in time for morning coffee from New York to Boulder, Colorado and all the way to Los Angeles. Pretty great, right? Let's take a look at what else this technology could do for customer service. We'll leave Amy behind and head to the Czech Republic.

146 Didymus, 2013

# IN THE MIDDLE OF NOWHERE

So you moved to a little cottage in the middle of nowhere. Congratulations! You're just five miles north of Vrchlabi, a small mountain town in the middle of Krkonose, the highest mountain range in the Czech Republic. They're hills compared to the Alps or the Andes, but these Czech mountains are known for harsh weather and tough winters. Today, two meters (6.56 feet) of snow covers the whole town and the surrounding cottages dotting the roads to the summit.

You fell in love with this place, but recently you've faced difficulties. You have a 20-year mortgage, and you borrowed money from your father to set up a private snowmobile chauffeur business for skiers but it hasn't really taken off yet, since last winter wasn't cold enough. You know this season will be better. It has to be! But you need an additional $150,000 (€129,000) to buy a new snowmobile and hire another driver. As kindling crackles in the fireplace, you're sitting on your sofa, sipping black tea and thinking: "I need a bank loan to get this business going."

It looks like any other local bank. There are large desks for meetings with financial advisors, and meeting rooms at the back of a large hall for private meetings. You pass through the hallway and enter one of the meeting rooms. There's a glass table and two stylish seats. In one of them sits a financial advisor in his forties with gray hair, horn-rimmed glasses, a bespoke navy blue suit and shiny brown leather shoes. "Thanks for meeting me on a Saturday," you say. "No problem," he responds, "I'm Mr. Prokop, your financial consultant. Let's discuss your credit options," he says, gesturing for you to sit in one of the cool seats.

Maybe you've already guessed. You haven't actually traveled from the snow-covered mountain village to a bank. They're all closed by now anyway. And Mr. Prokop isn't actually in that room.

It was 9 pm on a Saturday when you pulled on the Virtual Reality goggles you usually use for eliminating terrorists in the PlayStation game Medal of Honor. Then you turned on your connected game console and searched for the app to connect you with your bank. After a few powerful swings left and right with the remote control in your hand, you've opened the app you were looking for.

Your trip to the bank did and did not happen. Mr. Prokop exists and is indeed connecting with you on Saturday night, thanks to the bank's 24/7 consulting service, which they offer across the country. You have indeed visited a bank branch, but you've used your VR goggles and a game console with a virtual reality banking app connected to a virtual three-dimensional room to meet your financial advisor who connected from the comfort of his office in Prague using identical equipment. No driving. No need to check opening hours, since only one financial advisor is fully utilized by serving connecting customers from hundreds of miles away. And you get the same quality and availability of banking services. You have just used the latest possibilities of virtual reality to experience the banking of the future. That's just one more way technology will drastically change the way customers interact with companies in the very near future.

# CHAPTER SUMMARY

The future of customer service doesn't have to look so different from what we know today. But AI and transhuman technology will soon make the process much faster and easier. Typing responses 100 times faster, transmitting human knowledge to computers so others can use it, and having the ability to meet customers through virtual realityare only a few visions that may soon become reality. Customer service agents will work with far greater efficiency and customers will get personalized service at all hours of the day and night without leaving the comfort of their homes.

# CHAPTER 8

# THE IMPLE-
# MENTATION
# GUIDE

The last chapter looked at the future of AI and transhumanism and hypothesized about some of the amazing technologies that might soon be available. But the future is much closer than you probably realize. Mind sharing, brain uploading, telepathy and super-intelligence are still just theories. Transhuman customer service agents will vastly surpass the capabilities of humans in today's contact centers, but we're not quite there yet. This final chapter is dedicated to your pragmatic side, introducing a specific set of tactics to help you realize the full potential of the newest currently available technologies for customer service.

How can businesses leverage the potential of the newest AI and automation technologies? I mean right now, before an attractive female hologram assistant can open the door for you and listen to your grievances about the connectivity of a new smartphone, and before human agents equipped with telepathic chips attached to their heads read your mind as you think about the weird noise your car's brakes are making. How can businesses take advantage of recent technological breakthroughs?

In other words, how can businesses transition their customer service from the dehumanized age — filled with irritating voice automats and "no-reply" email messages — to the age of today's consumers who transfer money through Facebook Messenger, edit video files at the bus stop and play Pokémon GO augmented reality games with other fourteen-year olds in the park?

There's more than one possible approach. Investing a great deal of time into strategically transforming projects, rebuilding customer service operations from the ground up, re-hiring and re-training personnel and hiring pricy consultants to provide endless slideshows for board meetings is one option. Applying a lean, agile approach to customer service transformation is another. Taking a step-by-step approach, testing different ideas, failing forward through continuous learning curves defined by week-long development sprints, adding frequent result measurements and killing unsuccessful projects is a modern approach to putting new business ideas into practice.

**Tactics for implementing currently available transhuman customer service technologies:**

1. **Move old-fashioned email to chat and messengers**

2. **Replace contact forms with integrated in-app messaging**

3. **Implement smart contact forms with video chat and co-browsing**

4. **Implement a multichannel chatbot**

5. **Leverage new messaging channels**

6. **Boost agent productivity through Intelligent Advisor**

7. **Improve customer satisfaction and insights through integrations**

Here is a selection of proven tactics to leverage the potential of digital customer service by using currently available technologies. I've seen these tactics executed by Fortune 500 companies as well as quickly growing startups. This list is by no means exhaustive. Instead, it's a selection of often overlooked and under-appreciated tactics. Moreover, every company needs to first develop its own customer service strategy before considering implementing any of the following tactics.

# #1: MOVE OLD-FASHIONED EMAIL TO CHAT AND MESSENGERS

For a long time email was the leading digital customer service channel. Individual consumers and business customers used it to contact companies, and companies used it for internal communication. Many customer service experts still prefer email for resolving complex customer issues. A customer who faces a difficult and urgent problem without knowing exactly how to explain it to a customer service agent doesn't want to spend an hour typing a detailed email just to receive an automated response saying "Thank you, valued customer, we will get back to you in three days."

Email is like snail mail, only faster. It's great for lovers in long-distance relationships because they can stay connected across the world by exchanging romantic letters. It's great for lawyers who send multiple contracts and lengthy explanations to their clients. But when it comes to customer service, it's hard to think of a worse communication channel. It's bad for both customers and companies. It takes so long to write an email, and so long to read one. A certain type of customer sends a lengthy email full of irrelevant details just to explain that her phone has stopped sending text messages. Another type of customer sends a two-line email that requires the agent to ask 20 follow-up questions to identify the issue. And did you ever see a teenager opening their email and happily going through tons of spam and marketing messages? They use Snapchat, WhatsApp and Facebook Messenger instead.

The consumer-led shift from emails to social media and messaging has also inspired an increasing number of companies to downsize email as a customer service channel and to proactively invite customers to communicate with them on Facebook, Twitter and WhatsApp. KLM, the Dutch airliner, was the first in the world to place their social customer service team at a specially designated contact center in the middle of Schiphol airport in Amsterdam. Citibank, a 205-year-old old financial institution, began responding to their customers on Twitter back in 2009, only to be followed by thousands of other companies over the next few years. Strengthening live chat and messaging at the expense of email enables companies to save operational resources and improve sales conversions.

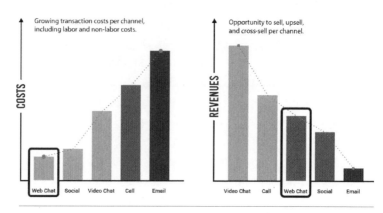

Cost vs. Revenue Potential of Live chat: Opportunity to sell, up-sell and cross-sell per channel", Brand Embassy, 2018

Ideally, integrating digital customer service into the legacy contact center will have positive effects for just about everyone in the company, from the agent to the CEO. Let's look more closely at who stands to benefit and why.

- **Customer Service Director**: Improved Average Handling Times (AHT) and overall operational efficiency is a benefit, as are the maintained levels of customer satisfaction.
- **CMO**: Increased online sales conversions in up-sales and cross-sales through real-time live chat as opposed to email, which sees lower sales conversions.
- **IT Director**: Using existing technology (live chat, Facebook Messenger) saves costs, as do the low extra implementation and maintenance fees. Costs for legacy email infrastructure are also cut.
- **CFO**: Increased online sales conversions and reduced overall operational expenses.

**RECOMMENDATIONS FOR IMPLEMENTATION**

If digital customer service has clear benefits for the entire company, what prevents you from accelerating your transformation? Implementing such strategies is typically a complex and difficult process. Allow me to provide some step-by-step recommendations for executing the digital customer service transformation.

- **Step 1**: Implement gradually by transferring email customer service traffic in phases. Start with small customer segments, then continue after processes and agents are operating efficiently.
- **Step 2**: Motivate customers to switch from email to real-time chat on their own by sending an active chat link initiating an instant live chat session with an expert agent. All the customer has to do is click on a link sent as a response to an email.
- **Step 3**: Encourage well-performing live chat agents to train and mentor newly assigned agents.

But it's important to realize that digital customer service integration isn't a silver bullet for your customer service woes. There are limitations.

**THE LIMITATIONS OF LIVE CHAT FOR CUSTOMER SERVICE**

Despite the advantages of digital customer service outlined above, some customers may still prefer to use email because they don't have any experience with live chat or they don't have social media profiles. But this doesn't mean digital customer service is irrelevant to them. On the contrary, even this type of customer has their place within the digital customer service ecosystem. The email addresses of these customers can be still routed to agents working with live chat so they can explain the benefits of using real-time chat while in conversation.

| | BENEFITS | SUCCESS MEASURES |
|---|---|---|
| CUSTOMER SERVICE | ↑ Operational Efficiency | ↓ Average Handling Time |
| MARKETING | ↑ Lead generation and online conversions | ↑ Online sales conversions |
| IT | ■ Leveraging existing technologies | ↓ Maintenance costs |
| FINANCE | ■ Improved cost management | ↓ OPEX<br>↑ Revenues |

Unless live chat and Facebook Messenger is optimized for the absolute majority of internet browsers, operating platforms and handheld devices, customers are likely to report decreased customer satisfaction. That's why choosing an IT partner and a customer service platform provider with an optimized solution is so important.

# #2: REPLACE CONTACT FORMS WITH INTEGRATED IN-APP MESSAGING

Today, the average iPhone user has between 60 and 90 apps installed on her phone.[147] People use apps for shopping, booking medical appointments, applying for a mortgage and streaming movies on their phones while commuting on the bus back home from a long day at work. Unlike what happens when you use email on one occasion, chat on another, and make a phone call some other time, your mobile apps are all sitting on your phone's home screen just a few millimeters from one another. They all work in a fairly similar way, and they all offer a pretty standardized user experience. And yet, when something goes wrong, like an error message pops up only a moment after your payment for new shoes was processed, the only chance for contacting customer service in the past was either calling a customer service hotline or opening a clunky web-based contact form. And of course, as if it weren't enough that your excitement about getting your shiny new sneakers right before the Friday party turned into frustration when the order got interrupted and the $149 (€129) disappeared from your bank account, you are now being asked to fill in all the personal and transaction information you already submitted. Damn! It almost seems like this company wants you to just shrug your shoulders and walk away. That's how difficult they're making it to fix a problem they caused in the first place!

147 Lovejoy, 2017

Mistakes happen, technical problems occur, transactions get interrupted. That's just a reality of doing daily business with thousands of customers who have hundreds of different devices, chip sets, screen resolutions, bank card issuers and product needs. But we should be done pushing the customer from one channel to another, making the entire process painfully slow and clunky.

In-app messaging enables consumers to interact with a human agent or a chatbot from within the mobile app while having the same user experience across the entire app. Messages are typically stored within the user's profile history, and conversations can be connected to the order history so the user doesn't have to leave the mobile app to resolve an issue. In order for a company to launch in-app messaging, they need to design an interface that's seamlessly integrated into an existing branded mobile app built on top of a messaging platform, typically using SDK, a software development kit. Then they have to connect it to a customer database (CRM System), and to a contact center response system by using API, an application program interface.

### WHY IMPLEMENT IN-APP MESSAGING?

Once again, the arguments for implementing this technology are clear and they go across the entire company.
- **Customer Service Director**: Decreased Average Handling Times (AHT) through more structured conversations with all necessary information in one place.
- **CMO**: In-app messaging leads to better customer experience, improving customer satisfaction scores.

Higher conversion rates in online sales are achieved through rich data format exchange capabilities, such as offering suitable products within conversations.

- **IT Director**: Easy implementation and maintenance compared to in-house solutions. One solution for all supported mobile platforms (iOS, Android, etc.) and screen resolutions.
- **CFO**: Increased online sales conversions and reduced churn. Cost-efficient implementation and long-term service subscription to an in-app messaging provider, compared to expensive and risky in-house development.

So, the benefits of technological implementation are clear. How can you make it happen?

## RECOMMENDATIONS FOR IMPLEMENTATION

- **Step 1**: Ask your digital customer service platform provider to integrate with your mobile in-app messaging. Do not use a separate platform just for in-app messaging.
- **Step 2**: Consider forming a task force team led by the department responsible for in-app messaging (typically marketing), the IT department responsible for implementation and integration, and the customer service platform partner responsible for integration with all other digital channels. Consider aligning development sprints (typically weekly or fortnightly) to minimize time to market for the go-live date.
- **Step 3**: Set up a prioritization and routing mechanism for incoming in-app messages. Integrate in-app messaging

into a unified queue with all other digital customer service channels.

- **Step 4**: Downscale your live chat capabilities or dedicated agents to reflect the higher demand for in-app messaging.
- **Step 5**: Set up smart self-service commands for customers joining the in-app conversation. This allows them to define the issue before the customer is assigned to the most appropriate agent.
- **Step 6**: Consider integrating in-app messaging with a chatbot that can also be used for social messaging and live chat, to automate the most frequent customer issues.
- **Step 7**: Implement step by step. Run a three-month pilot, carefully benchmarking key performance indicators across agent efficiency, customer satisfaction and sales with the previous solution (like a contact form) or a comparable channel (like a web-based live chat). Expand options and functionality over time.

# #3: IMPLEMENT SMART CONTACT FORMS WITH VIDEO CHAT AND CO-BROWSING

This is so common that it has probably happened to you. Sometimes our loved ones pass away, leaving us with a feeling of loss, but also with so much to do. Organizing the funeral, dealing with lawyers to resolve the will, and contacting electricity providers, gas providers, water providers, mobile operators, broadband and TV providers, and so much more. It's a painful process coming at the worst time when emotions are high, time is scarce and the last thing you want to do is spend hours filling in endless forms to change invoicing addresses or terminate contracts.

No wonder these contact forms aren't very popular. Many customers get disconnected and lose their data while spending ages looking for the last invoice number, the customer contact password or the last four digits of a credit card they no longer use.

Filling in a form with a total of 50 input fields spanning from basic personal contact information to scanning a photo of your electricity usage monitor display might easily take an hour. The form is typically divided into five to ten pages, each with a validating system that doesn't let you to proceed without submitting the requested information in the requested format. During the completion process, you are likely to get stuck several times and get interrupted by other activities.

Making this whole process considerably less painful while increasing submission rates is actually not very hard. The truth is, the company already knows a lot of the information you are requested to find or remember and then fill in. It's all sitting in their customer relationship management (CRM) system or their Enterprise Resource Planning systems (ERP). Submitting your name and password or any other type of unique identifier should be enough to pre-fill a large part of the form.

But what about the information you just can't find? Or what happens when you receive error messages saying

"Unknown format, please repeat."? For these purposes, you just click on a link that initiates a live video chat session with co-browsing capabilities, and the face of a friendly customer service agent pops up on the screen. After the agent greets you and asks permission, your internet browser screen gets shared with her as she navigates you through the process, giving advice on filling in the requested data and even pre-filling some of the fields for you, since she touch-types for living. What was once a painfully slow and irritating process is done in twenty minutes while you sip a cup of coffee. It's enough to make you believe in humanity again!

## ARGUMENTS FOR IMPLEMENTATION

- **Customer Service Director**: Improved agent utilization by assigning incoming video chats.
- **CMO**: Improved customer experience leading to higher submission rates.
- **IT Director**: Improved functionality of the website and modernization of the outdated form technologies with an integrated solution.
- **CFO**: Decreased churn rates (in the case of customer service forms) or higher revenues (in the case of sales contact forms).

**RECOMMENDATIONS FOR IMPLEMENTATION**

- **Step 1**: Build the implementation project in a lean way, divided into several stages. Integrate with the internal CRM/ERP system only at later stage, once the overall user experience of the contact form has been improved.
- **Step 2**: Integrate with a video chat solution that provides an easy-to-use experience for both the consumer and the agent. Enable the agent to initiate a co-browsing session with a customer anytime during the conversation. This decreases the level of uncertainty from using a new kind of communication channel.

**LIMITATIONS TO IMPLEMENTATION**

- Integration with legacy ERP/CRM systems without API layers might be challenging. A possible upgrade of the internal system might be required.
- The co-browsing experience needs to be implemented in a way that delivers the highest reasonable security and compliance. For example, credit card number masking needs to be implemented in banking services, and personal health data information needs to be masked in real-time in order to keep insurance customer privacy.

|  | BENEFITS | SUCCESS MEASURES |
|---|---|---|
| **CUSTOMER SERVICE** | ↑ Agent Utilization | ↑ Cases resolved<br>↓ Resolution times |
| **MARKETING** | ■ Improved Customer Experience | ↑ Contact submission rates |
| **IT** | ■ Improved website functionality<br>■ Integrated approach | ↓ Long-term maintenance costs |
| **FINANCE** | ■ Improved cost efficiency and revenues | ↓ Churn<br>↑ Revenues and profitability |

# #4: IMPLEMENT A MULTICHANNEL CHATBOT

What's all the fuss about chatbots lately? Mark Zuckerberg proclaimed at the F8 conference by Facebook in April 2016 that chatbots, robotic software programs designed to answer questions in a conversational mode almost like humans do, will soon be more popular than mobile apps and people will want to chat with bots the way they do with their buddies.[148] Moreover, Phil Libin, founder of Evernote, a successful technology company, and now Managing Director at General Catalyst, predicted that soon the number of bots will be similar to the number of mobile apps.[149]

148 Sharf, 2016
149 Top, 2016

Facebook Messenger is used by over 1.3 billion monthly active users,[150] and this number has multiplied by three within the last three years.[151] Over 100,000 bots have been built since early 2016, when the Bots for Messenger platform was launched. With over 10,000 software developers working on new chatbots every day, the number is likely to continue to rise.[152]

Some experts say that since chatbots are quicker to make and less expensive overall than for mobile apps, chatbots will secure a prominent place on the market, precisely at the moment when mobile apps are struggling to get downloads. But just how smart are chatbots today? To be honest, not very. Most of the chatbots out there remind me of the IVR technologies built in the '80s. "Select one to get your newest offerings, select nine to be connected with our rep." This sucks. I've already mentioned Tay, Microsoft's, flagship AI-powered chatbot, which caused an international public relations crisis. When let loose, it quickly began spreading racist and genocidal remarks.[153] Bad bot! No more tweeting for you, Tay!

But here's why I am excited to see more chatbots being launched every day:

- Chatbots help mobile operators and banks coping with signal outages or mobile/online banking outages to respond to tons of incoming questions very quickly. So

150 Constine, 2016
151 "Number of monthly active Facebook Messenger users from April 2014 to September 2017 in millions," 2018
152 Johnson, 2017
153 Price, 2016

people don't have to wonder why their Facebook wall isn't updating (I know the pain very well) or where their money went (almost as bad as the frozen Facebook wall, right?).

- Chatbots give consumers fast and relevant information about when their package will be delivered, or what happened with the availability of their eagerly awaited iPhone X. Without bots, they'd be waiting for days and way too often wouldn't get a response at all.
- Chatbots help companies that are notoriously unresponsive to customers improve their service just a bit by responding automatically. It's not an ideal solution, but in this case any improvement is better than nothing.

Thanks to chatbots, Intelligent Advisors and other AI-powered technologies, human contact center agents will be able to focus on more meaningful, complex tasks and conversations that require the most crucial thing: empathy. Don't forget, 82% of consumers think that companies could have done more and been more empathetic to avoid them leaving.[154] And 62 billion dollars were lost last year alone due to poor customer service, a figure that grew by $20 billion (€17.3 billion) in just three years![155] Humans still play an irreplaceable role in contact centers.

There's a bot for every purchase and customer complaint. They range from car co-pilot assistants you can use to play your favorite song while driving, to shopping assistants who tell you which shirt will complement your new Tom Ford skirt, to scheduling assistants that help you get

154 Kolodny, 2010
155 Hyken, 2017

a medical appointment, and even virtual customer service assistants. For customer service, we can narrow it down to the following use cases that can be implemented with technologies currently available on the market:

- Full-resolution automation through business process automation and chatbots
- Human agent augmentation through chatbots for messengers and chat
- Appointment scheduling

Let's take a look at each of them.

## FULL-RESOLUTION THROUGH BUSINESS PROCESS AUTOMATION

Here's how this might look in practice:
"Hi, it's Katie, how can I help you?"
"What's my current balance on my pre-paid SIM card please?"
"Wait a second, I will check it out for you." [5 seconds later]
"It's $14.90 (€13.00). Would you like to top up?"
"Yes please, let's do $20 (€17.30)."
"Right on. By the way, I see you often travel to Mexico. Would you like to turn on our roaming package for Mexico?"
"Well... I don't know. How much is it?"
"It's $9.90 (€8.50) per month. You can turn it on here anytime by typing 'Turn on Mexico roaming.'"
"Sound's good. I might do that."
"By the way, as an eager Spotify user, did you know you can stream your music now for free since Spotify is excluded from your data package?"

"I didn't know that! Cool!"

"Awesome. Well, Mary, anything else I can do for you today?"

"Nope, thanks, Katie."

"No problem, have a great afternoon in San Diego. Don't forget your sunglasses, looks like it's pretty sunny down there."

"Where are you, Katie?"

"Well, I'm actually everywhere and nowhere. I'm a bot built by the cool designers at Facebook in Palo Alto, CA. So let's call that my home, I guess."

Bots that complement human agents are especially useful for simple customer service use cases such as checking an account balance, topping up credit, paying an overdue bill, turning on a new service, or updating personal account data and preferences. The best way to start is to organize an internal design sprint among a small team of experts from marketing, customer service, online sales, customer experience and IT. Identify the top five to 15 use cases that can be resolved by a bot. Once a brief is drafted, an external technology partner can jump on the project and build the solution. It's important to make sure that the bot will be able to seamlessly transfer the customer to a human advisor at any point of the conversation. You don't want a bot frustrating your customers!

Many businesses start by launching human agent augmentation bots on Facebook Messenger. You can test them within a small and relatively safe group before expanding to live chat or other messaging platforms, or a mobile app. Depending on the business and industry, these easy-to-build and easy-to-implement chatbots could automate up to 50% of so-called first-level customer service issues. Projects like these might require a few weeks or a couple of months of cooperation between a bot provider and the internal IT department. Integration with internal systems is a must, as the bots pull data from personal accounts and process transactions directly from the conversational environment. If the bot isn't capable of resolving an issue, the system reports low resolution confidence and seamlessly transfers the customer to a human agent who picks up where the bot, like Katie, left off.

## HUMAN AGENT AUGMENTATION

Have you ever noticed that the stupidest problems always happen late at night or on weekends when customer service is unavailable? Murphy's Law is real! And if you're lucky enough to have your roaming cut out during working hours while you're traveling, you're going to wait on the line for 20 minutes, listening to that stupid Lady Gaga song over and over again. Murphy again, right? You can either scream, go for a coffee (or two) and get some rest, or you can go to Facebook Messenger, find your mobile operator's page and open up a conversation. Soon the simple process of selecting from a few options leads you to a step-by-step process to change your roaming settings and voilà, you're chatting with your mom in a few minutes! (During working hours? How dare you!).

Some might argue that these simple bots are just taking the not-so-intelligent IVR auto-responders from customer service hotlines into the friendly and human-powered social media environment. And that's true. Partially. Many bots launched recently are actually just bad copies of the all too familiar "Select one to get the newest offering, select nine to get connected to one of our friendly assistants." These are poor examples that may lead to decreased customer satisfaction as well as decreased customer experience. They may also endanger brand value, because dissatisfied social users are always only a few clicks away from causing a public relations crisis. Smart human agent augmentation is built around well-defined frequent customer service use cases, connecting easy-to-follow resolutions to frequently asked questions and properly created libraries of possible customer requests. These are then packaged into surprisingly friendly and easy-to-use chatbot conversations which enable customers to reach a resolution in a few clicks that take about a minute. That's an IVR killer, and a helping hand to the customer who desperately needs one on a Saturday night. Building a bot that can do all this takes about an hour and it can be set up to run the next day.

## APPOINTMENT BOOKING THROUGH CHATBOTS

I truly dislike picking up a phone and trying to get a hold of somebody on a landline. Not knowing who will pick up the phone. Them not knowing who's calling. Never being sure whether I'll reach somebody helpful and friendly I know, or some neurotic weirdo who was allowed to speak to customers by mistake. So no wonder the "schedule a GP appointment for next month" task in my to do list has been happily unresolved for a little over a year. My doctor has a few neighbors in the list, including "get a handyman to fix our living room lamps" and "schedule a barber before my wife mistakes me for Robinson Crusoe." Scheduling is a pain. Scheduling over the phone is a pain multiplied by a hundred. (And have you seen the recent demo of the Google scheduling assistant ordering a table in a restaurant over the phone? It was so awesome that many consider it fake.[156] Google itself said that "more work has to be done before it's ready."[157]

Scheduling and appointment-booking chatbots can do everything that a typical receptionist or nurse can. They can select the reason for your visit, select an available date and time, confirm your identity and there we go, a calendar invite displays in your calendar and your general practitioner, handyman and barber are all looking forward to seeing you (hopefully not all at the same time). There are additional benefits besides the consumer's saved time and the improved customer experience, because the business can save considerable expenses by letting their employees work on more meaningful activities than just picking up phones or responding to emails, checking a calendar and confirming your attendance. Let's be more human here, and let humans do tasks requiring a brain, while bots do the rest.

## ARGUMENTS FOR IMPLEMENTATION

- **Customer Service Director**: Improved agent utilization, improved operational cost efficiency, improved employee job satisfaction and retention through automation, and

156 Kosoff, 2018
157 Haselton, 2018

better utilization of human agent skills. Additionally, expanded operability to 24/7/365 without a necessary budget increase.

- **CMO**: Improved customer experience and increased online sales conversions or submission rates along with increased brand perception as an innovator by leveraging the most modern technology on the market.
- **IT Director**: Lowered IT resource allocation and lowered implementation costs (if done right) with a high impact on business efficiency and financial results.
- **CFO**: Maintained or lowered customer service headcounts.


**LIMITATIONS TO IMPLEMENTATION**

- Poorly designed chatbots can damage brand equity. Companies need to pay close attention to authentic language tonality, useful functionality and managing customer expectations.
- Chatbot projects need to be well-communicated internally as automation projects, which can make customer service agents feel anxious about the future of their jobs.

|  | BENEFITS | SUCCESS MEASURES |
|---|---|---|
| **CUSTOMER SERVICE** | ↑ Agent utilization<br>↑ Job Satisfaction<br>■ Expanded operability | ↓ Average Handling Time<br>↑ Cases resolved |
| **MARKETING** | ■ Improved Customer Experience<br>↑ Brand Equity | ↑ Generated Leads<br>↑ Online sales conversions |
| **IT** | ↑ Business efficiency through technology | ↓ Maintenance costs |
| **FINANCE** | ↑ Cost efficiency | ↓ Operational expenses |

# #5: LEVERAGE NEW MESSAGING CHANNELS

Could WhatsApp be an efficient customer service channel? The fact that you are reading about WhatsApp in a customer service book is the culmination of a very unlikely story. Two entrepreneurs, Brian Acton and Jan Koum, founded a small technology startup back in 2009 after one of them was denied a position at Facebook as a software developer. The same company bought WhatsApp only five years later for a mind-blowing $16 billion dollars (€13.8 billion). The company back then had only 55 employees, which makes it possibly the most efficient acquired company in history, with $350 million (€302 million) of return per head. Since early 2018, WhatsApp has offered its dedicated business solution for companies that want to expand their customer service to this popular messaging channel. Mexico, India, Indonesia,

UK and USA became the first countries where WhatsApp Business was offered, followed by other countries and technology providers the same year. The company claims that over 80% of small businesses in India communicate with their customers and grow their business through WhatsApp. If that's true, the business impact of WhatsApp on better customer service, higher online sales and improved customer satisfaction may be significant not only in India, but in all countries where WhatsApp has gained popularity.

But WhatsApp was never meant to be a customer service channel. Built to help teenagers communicate with their peers, WhatsApp has purposefully been kept simple. The founders have strictly avoided polluting the user experience with display ads or sponsored content. Brands were not welcomed as advertising sponsors, unlike with Twitter, Google+ and Facebook, whose business models are based on advertising revenue. In the case of Whatsapp, the company was not generating any revenue at the time of acquisition and even today there is no business model for generating revenues for what is currently the second-largest mobile messaging platform in the world.

Until recently, companies could directly respond to customers via WhatsApp on a one-to-one basis only. Imagine you have 1,000 customers calling your landline in your living room at the same time. That's what was happening. These customers expect to receive a response as quickly as Anna, your classmate, responds to a funny picture you just posted to her. Meaning: in seconds. And a bunch of contact center agents with access to WhatsApp are snowed under by an overload of requests even though they're responding as fast as they can. Meaning: in hours or days. Result: not cool. People on WhatsApp don't care about overloaded, understaffed contact centers or missing professional technologies. They want their problem resolved now.

Before the official WhatsApp Business solution is implemented on the market and made fully accessible to companies both large and small, companies will find ways to satisfy their social customers in alternative ways. There are technology providers that have built workarounds that enable businesses to respond to customers on WhatsApp from unified interface. However, these solutions, since they are unofficial and not approved by WhatsApp, are very likely to malfunction and are under threat of their service being suspended at any time. Still, there is a growing number of companies large and small that take advantage of such solutions to provide better customer service on the channels where their consumers are most comfortable.

Apple, the consumer technology company, has recently levelled up its business communication game and introduced Apple Business Chat. The business solution enables companies to push notifications, initiate proactive conversations and respond to incoming customer queries by using iMessage, the messaging that's available in all communication gadgets from Apple, such as the iPhone, iPad, Mac or the Apple Watch. Customers can schedule appointments with doctors, pay their bills or send customer service tickets without leaving their favorite messaging application. Apple Business Chat, like the WhatsApp business solution, is a very new product on the market and doesn't yet have useful case studies showing business benefits in practice. However I assume that many businesses targeting social and "digital native" customers will leverage these new channels to complement existing ones.

## ARGUMENTS FOR IMPLEMENTATION

- **Customer Service Director**: Decreased Average Handling Times (AHT) through more structured conversations with all necessary information in one place.
- **CMO**: Social messaging in the native apps preferred by consumers improves customer experience, leading to higher customer satisfaction. Higher conversion rates in online sales are achieved through rich data format exchange capabilities (such as appointment scheduling) and built-in payment systems (such as Apple Pay).
- **IT Director**: Easy implementation and maintenance compared to custom-made messaging solutions. One solution fully supports a number of devices (such as iPhone, iPad and iMac).
- **CFO**: Increased online sales conversions and reduced churn. Possibly also improved financial collections. Service costs relatively low.

|  | BENEFITS | SUCCESS MEASURES |
|---|---|---|
| **CUSTOMER SERVICE** | ■ Improved Omnichannel support experience | ↓ Average Handling Time<br>↑ Cases resolved |
| **MARKETING** | ■ Improved Customer Experience | ↑ Generated Leads<br>↑ Online sales conversions |
| **IT** | ↑ Business efficiency through technology | ↓ Maintenance costs compared to custom solutions |
| **FINANCE** | ■ Improved Cost efficiency and revenues | ↓ Customer churn<br>↑ Financial collection rates |

# #6: BOOST AGENT PRODUCTIVITY THROUGH INTELLIGENT ADVISOR

"Alexa, play my favorite music." "OK, Google, buy me some pizza." "Hey Siri, remind me of Dad's birthday when I get home." The age of personal assistants is coming. Every year, 29% more consumers use personal voice assistance, such as Alexa, Google Now, Cortana by Microsoft or Siri on Apple HomePod. Spending on the development of both hardware and software to empower these assistants with new technology is projected to grow by 46% to reach $16 Bn by 2021[158]. Admittedly, personal assistants have improved from the "Fun for hardcore geeks" to "Useful even for my mom" stage in only few years.

Just recently, I visited a friend of mine who proudly guided me through his new apartment full of cutting-edge technologies and the newest gadgets. Our discussion while sitting on bar seats in a loft-like kitchen with a beautiful view of his garden was occasionally interrupted by him shouting to the next room: "Alexa, skip this song!" "Alexa, volume down, we can't hear each other!" Meanwhile, I was thinking, "can't he just reach out for the remote control and do it himself?" But then I realized that only a few years ago, when my friend would have been desperately pushing buttons on a remote control which was, at that time, the newest technological miracle, I would have thought "why can't he

---

158 Pestanes P. & Gautier B., The Rise of Intelligent Voice Assistants,

just take ten steps and change the song manually?" It's not only technology that has been changing, it's also people and our expectations for technology.

Remember when you first saw people talking on a mobile phone on the street? It was weird, right? Something that had to be attached to a wire for so many years suddenly got liberated and people placed them in their briefcases (never mind how big and heavy the cell phones were back then!) and occasionally pulled them out, extended the telescopic antenna and started to chat on the street. Only 20 years have passed and today mobile phones are so much smaller, lighter, and more powerful. We are now living through the early days of personal assistants. In only 10 years we will look back to this current time and laugh about how dumb and clunky our personal assistants used to be. But for the time being, they are the closest thing to a personal executive assistant you can have without paying a $60,000 (€52,000) annual salary.

How can personal assistants help in customer service? First of all, Alexa, Siri and their virtual brothers and sisters can significantly decrease the number of incoming requests that reach contact center agents, while helping customers resolve their requests much faster. Isn't "Siri, what time will my parcel be delivered today?" much easier than searching for a telephone number that's lost in your email inbox, calling, waiting on the line and talking to an agent? And buying your late-night dinner after a busy day at work doesn't have to take 20 minutes of searching for the restaurant you like on Google, ordering food online, filling out your credit card details and waiting for the order to be confirmed. You just say "Hey, Google, buy me my favorite spaghetti" and there you go. The decision-making process that leads to a warm bowl of pasta on your table was just outsourced to a cloud-based computer that remembers your favorite restaurants, your favorite meals in these restaurants, and your ratings of the meals. It's also ready to use your stored credit card details and contact information. Sophistication simplified. Spaghetti on your table.

While individual consumers like yourself are increasingly taking advantage of the newest AI-powered personal assistants that are always one click away on your smartphone, contact center agents are still sitting at their desks in large open office spaces with 10-year old keyboards, small LCD screens and not much AI-powered software at their disposal. This trend is changing over time, however. Increasingly, some contact centers are using so-called Intelligent Advisors that are seamlessly integrated into their customer service platforms. This enables them to respond to complex customer queries much faster by having their responses drafted by a computer rather than a human. Searching through multiple entries in a knowledge base, compiling several data inputs to find the best solution for the individual customer request and preparing an easily understandable response is actually a computer's job, not a human's. All the analytical and writing skills are outsourced to a robot so the human agent can tweak the tonality of the conversation, add a few personal notes and send them in only a fraction of the time that would otherwise be needed. Intelligent Advisors help suggest responses to complex issues, and also prepare quick responses to hundreds of customers at the same time when a mobile signal outage hits a telco company or an online banking outage hits a banking company. This technology can also suggest how other agents have resolved similar issues in the past, thus helping the human agents provide higher-quality care.

## ARGUMENTS FOR IMPLEMENTATION

- **Customer Service Director**: Improved agent utilization by focusing on more complex and empathy – requiring issues, while drafting simple queries, or queries that require plenty of research are outsourced to intelligent advisors.
- **CMO**: No particular benefit for marketing, as intelligent advisors serve as a back-office tool for customer service operatives.
- **IT Director**: Modernization and the gradual replacement of old and clunky knowledge base systems by intelligent advisors lead to lower maintenance costs and better utilization of business intelligence.
- **CFO**: Maintained or lowered customer service headcounts due to improved productivity.

|  | BENEFITS | SUCCESS MEASURES |
|---|---|---|
| **CUSTOMER SERVICE** | ↑ Agent utilization <br> ↑ Job Satisfaction | ↓ Average Handling Time <br> ↑ Cases resolved |
| **MARKETING** | – | – |
| **IT** | ↑ Technology Modernization <br> ↑ Improved business intelligence | ↓ Maintenance costs |
| **FINANCE** | ↑ Cost efficiency | ↓ Operational expenses |

# #7: IMPROVE CUSTOMER SATISFACTION AND INSIGHTS THROUGH INTEGRATIONS

I know what you're thinking: "Wait a second! Are you going to talk about integrations now, you nerd? That's because the word "integration" reminds you of that bearded software engineer in a "Facebook fu**ed my marriage" t-shirt you spoke to during your rare visit to the IT department. Integrations are a boring, always failing black hole in IT budgets. "Unless you integrate this new system with our CRM via API, which gets integrated with our ERP to ensure that we meet our SLA and management KPI, your whole project and your seat within it will go to hell," says a knowledgeable IT manager while looking at your proposition to implement a new customer service platform. And you can't blame him, because organizations use hundreds of systems, each generating or processing different data sets, which results in a giant mess of customer data split over numerous databases, with some data contradicting each other and a lot of it being incomplete or confusing.

Integration means order. Integration means one customer profile, with one conversation history, one set of previous purchases and one overview of personal information giving the company a truthful image of who the customer is, what she wants and what she likes. A marketer setting up a new direct mail campaign uses complete customer data to send meaningful and relevant offers to a small database of customers with the same needs. A strategist using complete customer data adjusts pricing models to best fit individual customer preferences while generating nice profits for the company. And so importantly, customer service agents can now respond to a customer who previously reached out via phone, email and live chat with the same pressing problem, by saying "I'm sorry you had to try so many times, let me resolve the issue now for good." Customer data integration across all communication channels is not an option for businesses, but a necessity if you want to stay relevant for the consumer.

But where are we today?

Lara has a problem. Her broadband at home is painfully slow. No more watching the new episode of The Handmaid's Tale on HBO tonight. Damn! Even the photos on her Facebook wall are loading in slow motion, so the best she can do is guess what's going to be in the picture based on the funny comments already loaded below a blank photo frame. Lara calls her broadband provider. "Somebody to Love" by Queen starts playing into her left ear, which is pressed to her mobile phone. "Cool song, haven't heard it for so long," she thinks. Three minutes pass, and the cool song starts over again. Another three minutes pass and Freddie Mercury is no longer so cool. Dammit! Lara hits disconnect, finds the latest email from her broadband provider and hits "Reply," then quickly describes her problem. "It's gonna take more than two days before I hear from them," she thinks after she sends the email. Lara then opens her Twitter account while using her pricy mobile data package, finds the appropriate handle and sends a tweet: "My broadband is killing me, fix it pls @att! And your #customerservice is always busy."

Lara has contacted her broadband provider three times in one hour. How many times do you think she will be contacted back? You guessed it right. It's highly likely that the left hand doesn't know what the right hand is doing. Lara will get one call, one email and one tweet back. The tweet comes two hours later, the call back comes the day after and the email comes next Tuesday. A friendly agent named Josh asks Lara on the phone to provide her account number to start the resolution process, Kerrie requests that Lara fill in a short contact form by email and "Your Customer Support Team" on Twitter asks her to send them the last invoice number by private message. What the heck? Are these three agents even in the same room? (They are not. One is sitting in Austin, Texas, another is in Miami, Florida and poor Josh, actually named Ranjit after his grandad, is calling from New Delhi).

What's the problem here? Data and processes are not integrated. The system in the contact center screams: Lara 1 is calling! Lara 2 is sending an email! Lara 3 is sending us a tweet! Lara could easily get schizophrenia if she knew how many selves were floating through the customer databases of the companies she is dealing with. If all of Lara's data were integrated, the company would contact her back using the most convenient channel for her. Plus they'd respond faster and be ready to help, not ready to force another contact form on Lara. Integration is salvation for Lara, even if she doesn't know it.

## WHAT ARE THE USEFUL INTEGRATIONS IN CUSTOMER SERVICE?

Here are three examples of integrations that bring specific benefits to modern customer service operations:

One of the most useful, data integration can be achieved by pulling data from all contact center systems into a unified customer relationship database. Emails, tweets, incoming calls, chat messages, tickets saved by a retail agent after a customer visits a physical store are all stored in one database sorted by unique customer identifiers. This type of integration would make the schizophrenia of multiple customer accounts disappear. Although sometimes challenging ("How can I pair this Mike1897 on Facebook with Mike our customer?") or time-consuming ("Are you really asking your customer service agents to pair some profiles manually?"), it can and should be done. Contact centers of all sizes and volumes should have their customer data fully integrated.

Another useful integration comes with the so-called Unified Queue. This allows contact center operations to put all incoming customer requests into one queue regardless of channel, and then to distribute the requests based on multiple criteria to the most appropriate agent at the most convenient time. Requests are prioritized based on the type of request (Has somebody just missed her flight?), social influence (Is Madonna tweeting about our customer service?!) or urgency (Did the customer emphasize that she needs to have her dress for the wedding tomorrow?). After Priority is determined, customer requests are distributed (or routed) to the most appropriate agent based on availability (does this agent currently have the capacity to take one more customer and resolve the request within a few minutes?) and skills (does the agent have the knowledge and training to provide guidance on this issue?). Some companies are flirting with so-called Matchmaking Algorithms, which pair agents and customers by matching the socio-psychological profiles of customers to those of agents. Although these approaches are promising, the available results are so far questionable. Integration leading to a Unified Queue is useful for contact centers that already have so-called Fully Blended Agents, where one support agent picks up the phone, responds to emails, tweets or sends live chat messages within one work shift.

| **Contact centers of all sizes and volumes should have their customer data fully integrated.**

Integrating Chatbots and ERP (Enterprise Resource Planning) systems or billing systems (called BSS or OSS) enables businesses to automate some customer requests completely. Is Judy trying to top-up her phone and data package? Does Peter want to change his home address because he moved in with his girlfriend? Derek needs to check whether his salary landed in his bank account? All this can be done by connecting the chatbot used in live chat in the mobile app or on Facebook Messenger with the internally used business system. Although some of these integrations may take time and effort, the benefits of saving time for contact center agents and improving customer experience and the speed of responses typically outweigh the negatives.

## ARGUMENTS FOR IMPLEMENTATION

- **Customer Service Director**: Decreased Average Handling Time and increased productivity as agents spend less time searching through disintegrated customer profiles in various systems. Decreased number of cases requiring resolutions and complete removal of duplicated efforts as customer inquiries from various channels are paired into one customer case assigned to only one agent.
- **CMO**: Improved customer experience through better personalization and utilization of the full scope of relevant customer data, leading to higher customer satisfaction.
- **IT Director**: Lower long-term data warehouse and business intelligence costs, fewer system and database customizations and higher data quality positively affecting business efficiency and financial results.
- **CFO**: Improved customer churn, lowered IT costs.

| | BENEFITS | SUCCESS MEASURES |
|---|---|---|
| **CUSTOMER SERVICE** | ↑ Agent utilization<br>↑ Job Satisfaction<br>■ Expanded operability | ↓ Average Handling Time<br>↓ Incoming cases |
| **MARKETING** | ■ Improved Customer Experience<br>↑ Personalization | ↑ Customer satisfaction and NPS |
| **IT** | ↓ Customization<br>↑ Business efficiency | ↓ Maintenance costs |
| **FINANCE** | ↑ Cost efficiency | ↓ IT costs<br>■ Improved churn and profitability |

# IMPLEMENTING TRANSHUMAN CUSTOMER SERVICE

Recently, my company was tasked with launching a personalized customer service chatbot for one of the large mobile operators in Europe. Thousands of consumers were flooding the under-staffed contact center with urgent queries spanning from troubleshooting requests to questions about topping-up credit or adding roaming packages. The contact center director, unhappy about ever-increasing volumes of incoming queries combined with requests "from above" to cut more costs from a contact center already stripped to its bones, was seeking an innovative solution that would drastically improve operational efficiency. We put together a chatbot that tackled the five most frequent customer inquiry types and we designed a solution for handling them automatically with AI-powered chatbots that understand the customer's intents, guide them through the resolution process and ultimately provide business requirements without the necessity of involving a human person. That part was easy. However, when it came to implementation and the customer found out that several business departments and teams would need to be involved, the project nearly came to a sudden end.

Fast forward four weeks and the chatbot was launched and helping customers with their pressing issues. Four weeks! How was that possible? The company changed its approach to innovation. Management dedicated a small, flexible, expert team of agile software engineers led by a product manager, a business analyst, and a customer experience specialist. For the duration of the project they were completely detached from otherwise painfully slow corporate processes. Instead, they synchronized with the design sprints of the technology partner, worked closely side by side with the external software provider and were empowered to make their own decisions in moving the project forward until launch. Technology was an important part of the success of this project, but I am confident that without the flexible and agile approach and the very close cooperation between all partners fully dedicated to the initiative, the project may have ended up in the cemetery alongside hundreds of similar projects full of great intentions but bad executions.

**AGILITY IS KEY TO SUCCESS IN INNOVATION**

It's virtually impossible that the technological advances I've been outlining are going to slow down anytime soon. They're certainly not going to stop. Instead, the adoption time of new consumer technologies will continue to shorten. So companies need to become ever more agile to keep up. Not only that, but companies have to embrace change and be quick to adapt to any changes in customer behavior and communication.

While it took 30 years for the telephone to reach 50% market penetration, it took less than a decade for Instagram to do the same. The same goes for all of the leading social media and messaging channels invented over the past

15 years. The adoption time needed for new consumer technologies keeps decreasing. But at the exact same time, companies have remained much slower to adopt new technologies. That needs to change, and it will in any company that wants to remain relevant. Agility is key.

Transhuman customer service is the future. But it's not going to happen automatically. There are certain steps that every company needs to take to ensure that they'll be ahead of the curve, embracing the newest technologies to improve customer experience while improving customer retention and profits. However, integration projects require the coordination of many departments and partners, launching a chatbot takes time and money, and implementing new disruptive technologies takes guts. Rome was not built in a day and your transhuman customer service won't be either. What should companies do to minimize the risk that their projects will be rejected by a bad director or will never see the light of day at all?

It starts with proper online demos and A/B testing of new systems and technologies through trial periods or Proof of Concepts (POC). When it comes to new technologies that are now available and will continue to become available thanks to digital customer service, the future remains unwritten. We can't be sure of the innovations that are to come, but even more than that, every company has different needs and different customers who demand different levels of service. Demos and trials are key for testing new technologies before full adoption. They also give you a chance to test the waters, so to speak, by seeing how different customers react to different options.

Once you know which technologies you'll implement, you need to take an agile approach to implementation. I'd suggest short sprint periods of about two weeks, rather than relying on long-term projects. Development teams need to run like well-oiled machines and they need to be quick to change direction, but also always focused on the task at hand.

It's also vital that management takes an entrepreneurial approach, with step-by-step implementation, budgeting and POCs. This includes choosing cooperation over competition so that internal client teams, technology partners and consultancies work together. The future of digital customer service is wide open and that also means the company needs to be wide open with no information silos to slow things down.

One of the popular, yet often overlooked, approaches to developing and launching new software technology projects in a much faster and meaningful manner is called Scrum. Designed for teams of three to nine members who break their work into actions that can be completed within two to fourweek incremental projects called sprints, Scrum has found its way into many software startups where speed of innovation is the only way to survive cash-tight operations. However, large operations are increasingly adopting Scrum across their teams and departments. Enterprise-level Scrum methodologies have been developed recently. These are called Scrum of Scrums, Large-scale Scrum (LeSS), or Scale Agile Framework (SAFe). Although some experienced IT executives claim that agile development cannot be implemented into business-critical systems such as internet banking, billing or CRM, I claim the opposite. Implementing agile development gradually within the entire IT organization and increasingly within the company as a whole is the only way large enterprises can continue to thrive in a market increasingly ruled by more nimble and fast-moving startups and large technology companies that have managed to remain flexible even though they can hardly be called startups anymore.

# CHAPTER SUMMARY

Currently available technologies enable businesses to leverage the potential of transhuman customer service while preparing on exponentially improving technological capabilities coming in the upcoming years. Implementing the seven tactics, including effecvtive use of social messaging, chatbots, and Intelligent Advisors, introduced in the Implementation Guide, can significantly improve business operations and bottom lines. Companies need an agile approach and work closely with technology partners to accelerate the digital transformation.

# CONCLUSION, OR INTRODUCTION TO THE FUTURE

Well, here we are at the end of the book. Thank you for making it this far!

Rather than ending this book with a conclusion, I'd like to end it with an introduction to the future. After all, I wrote Customer Service in the Transhuman Age to start a conversation, not to end one. My inspiration has been to examine the past, think hard about the present and make educated guesses about what lies ahead. So here are a few questions I'd like to pose to you, dear reader, as we end our journey together through these pages.

**What is the ideal relationship between technology and customer service?**

**How do we stay informed about the possibilities and problematics of future technologies?**

**How can we each develop the capacities and characteristics that make human beings truly human— empathy, humor, creativity, love—and put them to work in our daily lives and careers?**

**What would we do if our jobs were taken over by AI?**

**How would we continue to find meaning, to develop skills and express passions, and to make a living? What can we do that's irreplaceable? How can we be more human?**

Finally, one thing is sure and there is no question about it: No matter what happens, the future shall be interesting.

# ACKNOWLEDGEMENTS

I would like to thank several people without whom this book would not have found its way into your hands: Stephan Delbos, a talented writer and editor; Jirina Dunkova, my executive assistant, who very quickly outgrew every role given to her and contributed hugely to this book with data research and general project management; Gustavo Bonnano, an Italian football player turned talented graphic designer who designed the book cover and the visual dividers; Hana Bermannova with Monika Soukalova, who made a sleek, beautiful book out of a basic document.

Special thanks go to the admirable industry experts who provided crucial feedback on an early draft: Adrian Mares, Eduardo Gallo, Maros Varga, Marko Bjedov, and Martin Benda. And my deepest gratitude to Laurent Philonenko, who contributed important comments and also the lively, informative Preface. Julian Raabe gave critical feedback, and our thought-provoking discussions gave me some inspiration for this book. There have been many others who contributed to the early stages of this project and I thank you all very much.

I have also been influenced by several people and their work over the past decade as I've been exploring the challenges, solutions and future of the customer service industry. Among many others I would like to mention Antonio Damasio, Daniel Svoboda, Daniele Casuccio, Daniel Kahneman, Amos Tversky, Dan Ariely, Jeff Berg, Jiri Pavlicek, and Nicolas De Kouchkovsky.

Without Damian Brhel, my business partner and co-founder at Brand Embassy, as well as the company's leadership team, I know I would not have had the privilege of spending hundreds of hours researching and writing this blogpost turned white paper turned book some 6,000 miles and 9 time zones away in beautiful San Diego, California.

For their ongoing love and support I thank my parents, Jana and Ivan, and my dear sister Veronika. Finally my gratitude and love go to my two dearest: Kristyna, my wife and best friend, who has navigated my life for more than 10 years and has given it meaning while being bombarded by my endless flow of ideas and plans, and who contributed immeasurably to this book, commenting on multiple drafts; and Vilik, my beloved son, who has given me more energy and excitement than any energy drink or triple-shot coffee (not that they haven't been useful too).

My last thank you goes to you, the reader.

Thank you.

**Vit Horky**
Prague, Czech Republic & San Diego, California
November, 2016 – October, 2018

# RESOURCES

Acemoglu, Daron and Robinson, James A. Why Nations Fail. New York: Crown Business, 2012.

Aghion, Philippe and Howitt, Peter. "Growth and Unemployment." The Review of Economic Studies. 61.3. July 1994. 477-494.

"AI Fund FAQ." The Knight Foundation. 2006. https://knightfoundation.org/aifund-faq. September 25, 2018.

Andreessen, Marc. "Why Software Is Eating the World." August 20, 2016. https://a16z.com/2016/08/20/why-software-is-eating-the-world/. June 7, 2018.

Bacon, Francis. The New Atlantis and The City of the Sun: Two Classic Utopias. New York: Dover Publications, 2003.

Basker, Emek. "Change at the checkout: Tracing the impact of a process innovation." The Journal of Industrial Economics. June 2015. Volume 63, Number 2.339-70.

Bauer, Harald and Patel, Mark and Veira, Jan "The Internet of Things: Sizing up the opportunity" McKinsey. December 2014 https://www.mckinsey.com/industries/semiconductors/our-insights/the-internet-of-things-sizing-up-the-opportunity. June 21, 2018

Berg, Jeff, et. al. "Winning the expectations game in customer care." McKinsey. September, 2016. https://www.mckinsey.com/business-functions/operations/our-insights/winning-the-expectations-game-in-customer-care. June 6, 2018.

Boden, Margaret A. The Creative Mind: Myths and Mechanisms. New York: Routledge, 2003.

Bool, Arlene C., Sale, Jonathan P. "Turnover and Voice in Philippine Call Centers." Ilera Directory. 2009. http://www.ilera-directory.org/15thworldcongress/files/papers/Track_2/Poster/CS2T_29_SALE.pdf. November 25, 2017.

Bostrom, Nick. "How Long Before Superintelligence?" Nickbostom.com. March 12, 2008. https://nickbostrom.com/superintelligence.html. June 6, 2018.

Bostrom, Nick. "What Happens When our Computers Get Smarter than We are?" TED. March 2015. https://www.ted.com/talks/nick_bostrom_what_happens_when_our_computers_get_smarter_than_we_are/up-next. June 6, 2018.

Brynjolfsson, Erik and McAfee, Andrew. Race Against the Machine. Cambridge: Digital Frontier Press, 2011.

Chandler, Alfred D. The Visible Hand: The Managerial Revolution in American Business. Cambridge: Harvard University Press, 1977.

Chomsky, Noam. "How Dangerous Is Artificial Intelligence?" YouTube. September 13, 2017. https://www.youtube.com/watch?v=HUp7tQISfj4. June 14, 2018.

Chui, Michael, et. al. "Where machines could replace humans—and where they can't (yet)." McKinsey. 2016. https://www.mckinsey.com/business-functions/digital-mckinsey/our-insights/where-machines-could-replace-humans-and-where-they-cant-yet. June 6, 2018.

Clifford, Catherine. "Facebook CEO Mark Zuckerberg: Elon Musk's doomsday AI predictions are 'pretty irresponsible.'" CNBC. July 24, 2017. https://www.cnbc.com/2017/07/24/mark-zuckerberg-elon-musks-doomsday-ai-predictions-are-irresponsible.html. June 14, 2018.

Cohan, Peter. "Google's Engineering Director: 32 Years To Digital Immortality." Forbes. June 20, 2013. https://www.forbes.com/sites/petercohan/2013/06/20/googles-engineering-director-32-years-to-digital-immortality. June 6, 2018.

Columbus, Louis. "2017 Roundup Of Internet Of Things Forecasts." Forbes. December 10, 2017. https://www.forbes.com/sites/louiscolumbus/2017/12/10/2017-roundup-of-internet-of-things-forecasts/#18becb181480. June 6, 2018.

Collins, Tim. "Doomsday AI will cause a nuclear war by 2040 that could DESTROY humanity, and there may be no way to prevent it." Mail Online. April 24, 2018. https://www.dailymail.co.uk/sciencetech/article-5651327/Doomsday-AI-cause-nuclear-war-2040-DESTROY-humanity.html. September 26, 2018.

Constine, Josh. "Facebook is building brain-computer interfaces for typing and skin-hearing." April 19, 2017. TechCrunch. https://techcrunch.com/2017/09/14/facebook-messenger-1-3-billion/. June 13, 2018.

Constine, Josh. "Facebook Messenger Day hits 70M daily users as the app reaches 1.3B monthlies." September 14, 2017. TechCrunch. https://techcrunch.com/2017/09/14/facebook-messenger-1-3-billion/. June 6, 2018.

Court, David, et. al. "The consumer decision journey." McKinsey. 2009 https://www.mckinsey.com/business-functions/marketing-and-sales/our-insights/the-consumer-decision-journey. June 6, 2018.

Crevier, Daniel. AI: The Tumultuous Search for Artificial Intelligence. New York: BasicBooks, 1993.

Delbos, Stephan. "The Power of Emotions in Customer Experience." Brand Embassy. https://www.brandembassy.com/resources-center/emotionswhitepaper. September 27, 2018.

Dorn, David, "The Growth of Low-Skill Service Jobs and the Polarization of the US Labor Market." American Economic Review. 103.5. August 2013.

Didymus, John Thomas. "Google's Ray Kurzweil: 'Mind upload' digital immortality by 2045." Digital Journal. June 20, 2013. http://www.digitaljournal.com/article/352787#ixzz5SIOGj1ZL. September 27, 2018.

Elazari, Keren. "Hackers are on the brink of launching a wave of AI attacks." Wired. December 28, 2017. https://www.wired.co.uk/article/hackers-ai-cyberattack-offensive. September 25, 2018.

Ferreira, Antonio. "China's AI Supremacy." Tech HQ. March 21, 2018. https://www.techhq.io/6647/chinas-ai-supremacy/. June 19, 2018.

Frey, Benedikt Carl and Osborne, Michael A. "The Future of Employment: How Susceptible Are Jobs to Computerisation?" Oxford Martin. September 17, 2013. https://www.oxfordmartin.ox.ac.uk/downloads/academic/The_Future_of_Employment.pdf. June 6, 2018.

Gibbs, Samuel. "AlphaZero AI beats champion chess program after teaching itself in four hours." The Guardian. December 7, 2017. https://www.theguardian.com/technology/2017/dec/07/alphazero-google-deepmind-ai-beats-champion-program-teaching-itself-to-play-four-hours. June 6, 2018.

Goldin, C., and L. F. Katz.. "The Origins of Technology-Skill. Complementarity." The Quarterly Journal of Economics 113.3. August 1998. 693–732.

Gordon, Robert J. "Is U.S. Economic Growth Over? Faltering Innovation Confronts The Six Headwinds." Research Gate. August, 2012. https://www.researchgate.net/publication/254435372_Is_US_Economic_Growth_Over_Faltering_Innovation_Confronts_The_Six_Headwinds. June 6, 2018.

Goos, Maarten and Manning, Alan. "Lousy and Lovely Jobs: The Rising Polarization of Work in Britain." Review of Economics and Statistics. 89.1. February 2007. 118-133.

Green, Chris. "The End of Moore's Law? Why the Theory that Computer Processors Will Double in Power Every Two Years May Be Becoming Obsolete." The Independent. July 17, 2015. https://www.independent.co.uk/life-style/gadgets-and-tech/news/the-end-of-moores-law-why-the-theory-that-computer-processors-will-double-in-power-every-two-years-10394659.html. June 14, 2018.

Grimm, David and Miller, Greg. "Is a Dolphin a Person?" Science. February 21, 2010. http://www.sciencemag.org/news/2010/02/dolphin-person. June 6, 2018.

Haas, Benjamin. :"'Killer robots': AI experts call for boycott over lab at South Korea university." The Guardian. April 5, 2018. https://www.theguardian.com/technology/2018/apr/05/killer-robots-south-korea-university-boycott-artifical-intelligence-hanwha. September 27, 2018.

Haldane, J. B. S. Daedalus; or, Science and the Future. London: Kegan Paul, Trench, Trubner & Co, 1926.

Harris, Mark. "Obama honours IBM supercomputer." Tech Radar. September 18, 2009. June 6, 2018.

Haselton, Todd. "Google's Assistant is getting so smart it can place phone calls and humans think it's real." CNBC. May 8, 2018. https://www.cnbc.com/2018/05/08/googles-assistant-will-soon-place-phone-calls-to-book-appointments.html. June 19, 2018.

Higgins, Chris. "A Brief History of Deep Blue, IBM's Chess Computer." Mental Floss. July 29, 2017. http://mentalfloss.com/article/503178/brief-history-deep-blue-ibms-chess-computer. June 12, 2018.

Hsieh, Tony. Delivering Happiness: A Path to Passion, Profits and Purpose. New York: Grand Central Publishing, 2013.

Iozzio, Corinne. "Scientists Prove That Telepathic Communication Is Within Reach." The Smithsonian. October 2, 2014. https://www.smithsonianmag.com/innovation/scientists-prove-that-telepathic-communication-is-within-reach-180952868/. June 6, 2018.

Ito, Joi. "The Paradox of Universal Basic Income." Wired. February 29, 2018. https://www.wired.com/story/the-paradox-of-universal-basic-income/. June 13, 2018.

Johnson, Khari. "Facebook Messenger hits 100,000 bots." VentureBeat. April 18, 2017. https://venturebeat.com/2017/04/18/facebook-messenger-hits-100000-bots/. June 6, 2018.

Kahneman, Daniel, et al. Judgment Under Uncertainty: Heuristics and Biases. Cambridge: Press Syndicate of the University of Cambridge, 1982.

Kharpal, Arjun. "Stephen Hawking says A.I. could be 'worst event in the history of our civilization.'" CNBC. November 6, 2017. https://www.cnbc.com/2017/11/06/stephen-hawking-ai-could-be-worst-event-in-civilization.html. June 6, 2018.

Kolodny, Lora. "Study: 82% Of U.S. Consumers Bail On Brands After Bad Customer Service." TechCrunch. October 3, 2010. https://techcrunch.com/2010/10/13/customer-service-rightnow/. June 6, 2018.

Kosoff, Maya. "Uh, Did Google Fake its Big A.I. Demo?" Vanity Fair. May 17, 2018. https://www.vanityfair.com/news/2018/05/uh-did-google-fake-its-big-ai-demo. June 19, 2018.

Krueger, Alan. "How Computers Have Changed the Wage Structure: Evidence from Microdata, 1984–1989." The Quarterly Journal of Economics. 108.1. 1993. 33-60.

Kurzweil, Ray. "Google's genius futurist has one theory that he says will rule the future — and it's a little terrifying." Business Insider. May 2015. http://www.businessinsider.com/ray-kurzweil-law-of-accelerating-returns-2015-5. June 6, 2018.

Locke, Susannah. "Telepathy is now possible using current technology." Vox. November 9, 2014. https://www.vox.com/2014/11/9/7181029/telepathy-brain-communication. June 6, 2018.

Lovejoy, Ben. "The average smartphone user spends 2h 15m a day using apps — how about you?" 9 to 5 Mac. May 5, 2017. https://9to5mac.com/2017/05/05/average-app-user-per-day/. June 6, 2018.

Manyika, James, et. al. "Disruptive technologies: Advances that will transform life, business, and the global economy." McKinsey Global Institute. 2013. https://www.mckinsey.com/~/media/McKinsey/Business%20Functions/McKinsey%20Digital/Our%20Insights/Disruptive%20technologies/MGI_Disruptive_technologies_Full_report_May2013.ashx. June 6, 2018.

McDermott, John. "Mobile Ads More Disruptive Than TV Spots." Ad Age. December 12, 2012. http://adage.com/article/digital/mobile-ads-disruptive-television-spots/238730/. June 6, 2018.

Mokyr, Joel. The Lever of Riches: Technological Creativity and Economic Progress. New York: Oxford University Press, 1990.

More, Max. "Transhumanism and the Singularity." Humanity Plus. http://humanityplus.org/philosophy/philosophy-2/. June 6, 2018.

Nietzsche, Friedrich. Thus Spake Zarathustra. Project Gutenberg. https://www.gutenberg.org/files/1998/1998-h/1998-h.htm. June 6, 2018.

Nilsson, G. "Brain and body oxygen requirements of Gnathonemus petersii, a fish with an exceptionally large brain." Journal of Experimental Biology. 1996. 199: 603-607.

Nordhaus, William D. "A Review of the 'Stern Review on the Economics of Climate Change.'" Journal of Economic Literature. Vol. 45, No. 3 (Sep., 2007), 686-702.

Ordy, J. M. Neurobiology of Aging: An Interdisciplinary Life-span Approach. New York: Plenum Press, 1975.

Pena, Aurelio A. GMA News Online. "RP call centers reel from world's highest turnover." March 20, 2008. http://www.gmanetwork.com/news/news/specialreports/85640/rp-call-centers-reel-from-world-s-highest-turnover/story/. November 25, 2017.

Phua, C., et al. A comprehensive survey of data mining-based fraud detection research. https://arxiv.org/pdf/1009.6119.pdf. June 6, 2018.

Pickrell, John. Timeline: Human Evolution. New Scientist. September 4, 2006. https://www.newscientist.com/article/dn9989-timeline-human-evolution/. June 6, 2018.

Plaksij, Zarema. "Customer Churn: 12 Ways to Stop Churn Immediately." Super Office. March 7, 2018. https://www.superoffice.com/blog/reduce-customer-churn/. June 6, 2018.

Price, Rob. "Microsoft is deleting its AI chatbot's incredibly racist tweets." Business Insider. March 24, 2016. http://www.businessinsider.com/microsoft-deletes-racist-genocidal-tweets-from-ai-chatbot-tay-2016-3. June 6, 2018.

Regalado, Antonio. "With Neuralink, Elon Musk Promises Human-to-Human Telepathy. Don't Believe It." MIT Technology Review. April 22, 2017. https://www.wired.com/story/musk-model-3-tesla-production-delays-january/. June 6, 2018.

Roser, Max and Ortiz-Ospina, Esteban. "World Population Growth." Our World in Data. April, 2017. https://ourworldindata.org/world-population-growth. June 6, 2018.

Sandberg, Anders and Bostrom, Nick. "Whole Brain Emulation: A Roadmap." Technical Report #2008 3. Future of Humanity Institute. April 5, 2009.

Sanders, G.I. "Employee Productivity Statistics: Every Stat You Need To Know." Dynamic Signal. April 21, 2017. https://dynamicsignal.com/2017/04/21/employee-productivity-statistics-every-stat-need-know/. June 19, 2018.

Seetharaman, Deepa. "Russian-Backed Facebook Accounts Staged Events Around Divisive Issues." The Wall Street Journal. October 30, 2017. https://www.wsj.com/articles/russian-backed-facebook-accounts-organized-events-on-all-sides-of-polarizing-issues-1509355801. September 25, 2018.

Magids, Scott et al., "What Separates the Best Customers from the Merely Satisfied." Harvard Business Review. December 03, 2015. https://hbr.org/2015/12/what-separates-the-best-customers-from-the-merely-satisfied. September 24, 2018.

Picard, R.W. Affective Computing. M.I.T Media Laboratory Perceptual Computing Section Technical Report No. 321 The MIT Press; Reprint edition 2000

Schumpeter, Joseph A. Capitalism, Socialism, and Democracy. New York: Harper Perennial, 1962.

Sharf, Samantha. "Look Here For A Glimpse At Facebook's Chatbot Future." Forbes. April 18, 2016. https://www.forbes.com/sites/samanthasharf/2016/04/18/look-here-for-a-glimpse-at-facebooks-chatbot-future. June 6, 2018.

Shanahan, Murray. The Technological Singularity. Cambridge: MIT Press, 2015.

Stewart, James B. "Facebook Has 50 Minutes of Your Time Each Day. It Wants More." The New York Times. May 5, 2016. https://www.nytimes.com/2016/05/06/business/facebook-bends-the-rules-of-audience-engagement-to-its-advantage.html?_r=0. June 6, 2018.

Swinscoe, Adrian. "The Longest Lasting Emotions in Customer Experience." Forbes. November 11, 2014. https://www.forbes.com/sites/adrianswinscoe/2014/11/11/the-longest-lasting-emotions-in-customer-experience/#8bea5585e40a. June 13, 2018.

Temperton, "'Now I am become Death, the destroyer of worlds.' The story of Oppenheimer's infamous quote." Wired. August 9, 2017. http://www.wired.co.uk/article/manhattan-project-robert-oppenheimer. June 19, 2018.

Titcomb, James. Mark Zuckerberg confirms Facebook is working on mind-reading technology. April 19, 2017. The Telegraph. http://www.telegraph.co.uk/technology/2017/04/19/mark-zuckerberg-confirms-facebook-working-mind-reading-technology/. June 6, 2018.

Top, Derek. "Intelligent Assistants Conference San Francisco 2016 – Agenda & Presentations." Opus Research. September 16, 2016. http://opusresearch.net/wordpress/2016/09/16/intelligent-assistants-conference-san-francisco-2016-agenda-presentations/. June 6, 2018.

Urban, Time. "The AI Revolution: The Road to Superintelligence." Wait But Why Blog. January 22, 2015. https://waitbutwhy.com/2015/01/artificial-intelligence-revolution-1.html. June 18, 2018.

Vinge, Victor. "The Coming Technological Singularity: How to Survive in the Post-Human Era." 1993. https://edoras.sdsu.edu/~vinge/misc/singularity.html. June 14, 2018.

Vinge, Vernor. "What Is the Singularity?" Mindstalk. 1993. http://mindstalk.net/vinge/vinge-sing.html. June 6, 2018.

Wiant, Wade. "Contact Center 2020: Are You Prepared?" ICMI. April 4, 2016. https://www.icmi.com/Resources/Strategy-and-Planning/2016/04/Contact-Center-2020-Are-You-Prepared. June 6, 2018.

Wood, Bernard. "Fifty Years After Homo habilis." Nature. April 3, 2014. 31–33.

Yoshida, E., Ge, Yoshida E. "Social Robotics." 9th International Conference ICSR 2017, Tsukuba, Japan. November 22-24, 2017. Proceedings.https://www.springer.com/gp/book/9783319700212. June 6, 2018.

"A Look at How Assortment Can Drive Success in Today's Retail Environment." NRF. March 13, 2018. https://nrf.com/who-we-are/retail-communities/digital-retail-shoporg/state-of-retailing-online. June 14, 2018.

"Artificial Intelligence." The European Commission. March 2, 2018. https://ec.europa.eu/digital-single-market/en/artificial-intelligence. June 19, 2018.

"Business process outsourcing industry worldwide—Statistics & Facts." Statista. https://www.statista.com/topics/2257/business-process-outsourcing-industry-worldwide/. June 6, 2018.

"Case Study: Transforming the CX approach to meet the demand for digital customer interactions." Brand Embassy. 2018

"Gartner Says Organizations Are Changing Their Customer Experience Priorities." Gartner. June 9, 2015. https://www.gartner.com/newsroom/id/3072017. June 6, 2018.

Global Contact Center Survey 2017. Deloitte. https://www2.deloitte.com/us/en/pages/operations/articles/global-contact-center-survey.html. June 9, 2018.

"How T-Mobile Delivers Human-Centric Social Customer Service with Brand Embassy." Brand Embassy. 2018. https://www.brandembassy.com/resources-center/socialsidetmobile. June 14, 2018.

"Julian Huxley and Transhumanism." Huxley.net. https://www.huxley.net/transhumanism/index.html. June 6, 2018.

"Life Expectancy by Age, 1850–2011." Info Please. https://www.infoplease.com/us/mortality/life-expectancy-age-1850-2011. June 6, 2018.

"Median Call Center and Customer Service Executive Salary in India." PayScale. https://www.payscale.com/research/IN/Job=Call_Center_and_Customer_Service_Executive/Salary. November 25, 2017.

"Membership and Applicant Growth." Alcor. http://www.alcor.org/AboutAlcor/membershipstats.html. December 5, 2017.

"National Average Cashier Salary in USA." Payscale. https://www.payscale. com/research/US/Job=Cashier/Hourly_Rate. November 25, 2017.

"Number of mobile app hours per smartphone and tablet app user in the United States in June 2016, by age group." Statistica. https://www.statista.com/ statistics/323522/us-user-mobile-app-engagement-age/. June 6, 2018.

"Number of monthly active Facebook Messenger users from April 2014 to September 2017 (in millions)." Statistica. 2018. https://www.statista.com/ statistics/417295/facebook-messenger-monthly-active-users/. June 6, 2018.

Pestanes P. & gautier B. "The Rise of Intelligent Voice Assistants" Wavestone https://www.wavestone.com/app/uploads/2017/09/Assistants-vocaux-ang-02-.pdf

"Průměrný hrubý měsíčny plat pro Česká republika." Platy.cz. https://www. platy.cz/platy/zakaznicka-podpora/specialista-podpory-zakazniku. June 14, 2018.

"State of Retailing Online." NRF. https://nrf.com/who-we-are/retail-communities/digital-retail-shoporg/state-of-retailing-online. June 6, 2018.

"System/370 Announcement." IBM. June 30, 1970. http://www-03.ibm.com/ ibm/history/exhibits/mainframe/mainframe_PR370.html. June 6, 2018.

"The Big Mac Index." The Economist. January 17, 2018. https://www.economist. com/content/big-mac-index. June 14, 2018.

"UN projects world population to reach 8.5 billion by 2030, driven by growth in developing countries." The United Nations. July 29, 2015. https://www.un.org/ sustainabledevelopment/blog/2015/07/un-projects-world-population-to-reach-8-5-billion-by-2030-driven-by-growth-in-developing-countries/. June 6, 2018.

"U.S. Games 360 Report: 2018." Snip.ly. May 24, 2018. http://snip.ly/ gnmsh#http://www.nielsen.com/us/en.html. June 6, 2018.

"What Is Horizon 2020?" The European Commission. 2014. https://ec.europa. eu/programmes/horizon2020/what-horizon-2020. September 25, 2018.

"Woody Allen: his 40 best one-liners." The Telegraph. May 5, 2017. https://www. telegraph.co.uk/comedy/comedians/woody-allen-best-jokes-and-one-liners/woody-allen14/. June 14, 2018.

"50 Years of Moore's Law." Intel. https://www.intel.com/content/www/us/en/ silicon-innovations/moores-law-technology.html. June 6, 2018.

"69 Percent of Jobs in India Threatened by Automation: World Bank." The Quint. October 5, 2016. https://www.thequint.com/news/hot-news/69-percent-of-jobs-in-india-threatened-by-automation-world-bank. June 19, 2018.

**VIT HORKY**
**CUSTOMER SERVICE IN THE TRANSHUMAN AGE**

Published by:
Brand Embassy Ltd, odštěpný závod, Rohanské
nábřeží 678/25, 186 00 Prague 8, Czech Republic

© Vit Horky 2018
Editor: Stephan Delbos
Design: Gustavo Bonnano
Typography: Hana Bermannova, Monika Soukalova
First edition, 2018
ISBN 9781731082152

Printed in Great Britain
by Amazon